THE MASTER ARCHITECT SERIES V

PERKINS & WILL

Selected and
Current Works

First published in Australia in 2000 by
The Images Publishing Group Pty Ltd
ACN 059 734 431
6 Bastow Place, Mulgrave, Victoria, 3170
Telephone (61 3) 9561 5544 Facsimile (61 3) 9561 4860

National Library of Australia Cataloguing-in-Publication Data

Perkins & Will: selected and current works.

Bibliography.
Includes index.
ISBN 1 86470 064 5
ISSN 1320-7253

1. Perkins & Will. 2. Architecture, Modern—20th
century—United States. 3. Architects—United States.
(Series: Master architect series V).

720.97

Edited by Renée Otmar, Otmar Miller Consultancy Pty Ltd
Designed by The Graphic Image Studio Pty Ltd,
Mulgrave, Australia
Printed in Hong Kong

Contents

Introduction

A Larger Context

In the 65 years since Lawrence B. Perkins and Philip Will, Jr. established Perkins & Will, we have been working to explore a particular type of architectural practice—a practice focused not only on the client program, but also on the larger social context in which the project will make its lasting contribution. Civic commissions—schools, colleges, city centers—have demanded searching innovation and now anchor a Perkins & Will design tradition that extends from the 1938 Crow Island School to the 2000 International School of Manila. Our practice is the result of a concept of service that centers on the overall aspirations, both built and intangible, of each client; a successful project aligns architecture and planning with the widest definition of the client's interests. In this sense, the context of a project always includes the organizational goals of its owner. In order to deliver an architecture that anticipates and responds to the functional, societal, and dynamic institutional elements of each project, Perkins & Will has evolved a firm culture of collaboration and shared expertise. The work included in this volume is the product of many talented and dedicated individuals who bring their skills to our group exploration.

Our Design Tradition

In describing a body of work as large as the one in this volume, it is tempting to try to single out stylistic constants, and to focus on the similarities of the buildings. Naturally, we all like to be able to understand architecture in terms of similarities, thematic rhymes and repetitions that help to characterize and relate groups of buildings. We enjoy recognizing signature materials or colors, recurring elevation compositions; we like to identify a building by familiar features that place it within a tradition we already know.

Many of the formal themes in Perkins & Will's design portfolio derive from a clean, restrained Modernism. The architectural language of our projects has often blended a uniquely Midwestern sense of horizontality with interwoven, perpendicular elements. Many plan layouts, in particular those for complex programmatic buildings, have been carefully dissolved into intriguing dis-assemblies that reveal their functions and hierarchical relationships. The unbundled organization of these buildings into miniature campuses creates complementary outdoor spaces integral to their overall composition and function.

But there are undeniable *dis-similarities* in this volume of work which are just as important to Perkins & Will's design tradition. The social art of architecture, as Ralph Johnson expresses it, is of crucial significance to us, and it inevitably leads to particularization of each project for its site and function. In the first instance, social architecture creates buildings that are good civic neighbors. Their site strategies, formal compositions, and environmental sensitivity take into account their contexts. Urban architecture always has an opportunity to extend or heal the surrounding fabric; suburban and rural architecture always affects its local topography, vegetation, and climate—for better or worse. Design strategies are influenced by specific contexts and particular expressions of cultural diversity in all Perkins & Will's international projects, as well as in projects such as the Desert View Elementary School and the Tarry Research and Education Building at Northwestern University.

Perkins & Will is also devoted to a tradition of social architecture in our series of commissions for institutions of key social importance. Schools, civic centers, and museums offer the opportunity to express in built form the value society has for centuries placed on these foundations. We are mindful that a civic project serves not only the individual (perhaps temporary) commission or client, but also the more permanent community at large. When we can express the kernel of civic importance in an architectural form that enriches its archetype, then we can create "architectural symbols of contemporary civic life."[1] This is one role of architecture in working to "make modern life more meaningful and reaffirm our cultural values."[2]

Finally, our social architecture derives from a long-standing faith in program-driven design. When Larry Perkins literally went to school with children in order to tailor his design to their needs, he demonstrated an intense commitment to the client's and user's point of view. Today, we still believe that whenever we borrow the client's perspective and actively use it to define the building, we find a clarity that remains invisible otherwise. Design produced by the social interaction of users and architects seeking the program together uniquely integrates architecture with our clients' missions.

Service to Our Clients

Larry Perkins expressed our continuing sense of the relationship between design and service when he wrote that "the applause we seek is the quiet trust and satisfaction of clients and public who know that their interests have been thoughtfully served."[3] When an architect devotes his or her creative skills first to comprehending the client's overall goals—financial restraints, social mission, competitive challenges, opportunities for expansion, and the cultural and economic legacy he or she is creating—as well as the client's building goals, then design can fulfill the client's best interests. When the architect also expands his or her charge to consider the implications of the client's program on the surrounding community, then design inevitably reflects the public's best interests. Thoughtful service means balancing all these agendas in the building.

The most difficult project for a student in an architectural studio is one set on a blank site. Contextual restraints paradoxically produce the most interesting and imaginative solutions. We consider the client's and the public's interests as much a part of a project's context as site conditions. These additional factors enrich the architecture, and prepare it for longer and more relevant use. When we have met situations where clients were best served by not building at all, we have urged frugality, patience, renovation. When we have met clients whose work situations demanded designers on-site, we have opened new, project-specific offices. The challenge of responding to each new set of circumstances belonging to a particular client, site or program calls for a flexibility that frees up design possibilities. We would no more assume a standard business or operations model for a client than we would apply a tired, preconceived formal plan layout to his or her program. Each situation asks us to forge a distinct relationship and a new solution.

Our Firm Culture

The opportunity to serve a wide variety of clients has led to dramatic changes in the physical structure of Perkins & Will's offices, and to an evolution of our firm culture. In the past five years, we have grown to eight offices housing more than 500 architects, planners, and interior designers. The pool of talent represented by so many carefully trained professionals is our biggest asset; marshalling and applying this talent properly is one of our biggest challenges.

In order to take fullest advantage of imagination and expertise wherever it resides inside our national offices, Perkins & Will has created virtual Centers of Excellence: groups of Perkins & Will professionals with specialized expertise in a given client or market type. These Centers act as resource banks of project-specific intelligence, so that we can have immediate access to an employee's talents and make him or her available to a given project, no matter where he or she is physically located. The success of the Centers depends directly on other staples of the Perkins & Will workplace: internal collaboration and teamwork, responsiveness, responsibility. We have found that we can offer clients only what we offer each other as co-designers: respect, the ability to listen, fairness, and patience.

We are actively developing technological tools to help us extend the reach of these very personal attributes across the geographical divides which separate Miami, Minneapolis, Santa Monica, Chicago, Atlanta, Charlotte, Pasadena, and New York. Intranet sites help to keep employees aware of staff and organizational changes in sister offices; linked CAD software makes it possible to produce drawings simultaneously in multiple sites; and e-mail is used to forward general queries and news of project successes. Extranet sites now allow our clients unprecedented access and input to our work as it progresses. We also find new technological applications for expanded services that complement our traditional planning, architecture, and interior design: life-cycle costing, workflow/workplace redesign, code compliance assessments, facility inventory, strategic and operations analysis, equipment planning, feasibility studies etc.

Conclusion

As we move into the 21st century, Perkins & Will is proud to carry forward the legacy of the past 65 years in our search for design excellence, our tradition of comprehensive service to both clients and the public, and our firm's culture of individual respect. This volume presents work produced as our vision of the present; as the future broadens, we look forward to project contexts that have ever wider implications.

[1] Ralph Johnson, "Introduction," in *Ralph Johnson/ Perkins & Will; Normative Modernism.* Milan: L'Arca Edizioni, 1998, p. 5.

[2] ibid., p. 6.

[3] Lawrence B. Perkins, "A Statement," in *Perkins & Will: The First Fifty Years.*

Schools

Desert View Elementary School

Design/Completion 1985/1988
Sunland Park, New Mexico
Gadsden Independent School District
44,000 square feet
Masonry bearing walls and exposed steel structure
Concrete block, steel, standing seam metal roofs, translucent
fiberglass roofs and canvas awnings at exterior walkways

This elementary school, for 800 kindergarten through sixth grade students, is one of three schools built in the area and based on a prototypical design. The three sites lie between a fragmented residential area and the railroad tracks that mark the border between New Mexico and Mexico in this semi-desert terrain. In response to the town's lack of identifiable center, the project's strong hierarchical form creates a focal point for the community. At the level of the educational community, the school is conceived of as an ideal village, created by clusters of classrooms and shared spaces arranged around open courtyards of varying scales.

Each functional type is housed in a different formal building type and arranged hierarchically and axially within the circular stone wall which separates the precinct of the school from the untouched desert beyond. Sheds enclose the repetitive classroom units; larger-scale pavilions house the dining and multipurpose room; parallel walls with punched windows and clerestory roofs

Continued

1

0   100   200ft   N

2

3

4

5

6

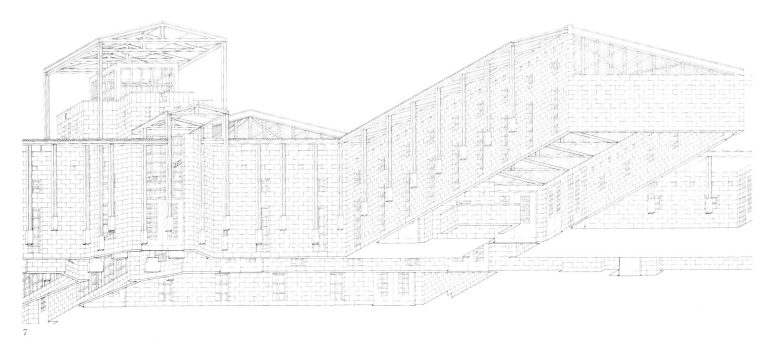

7

8

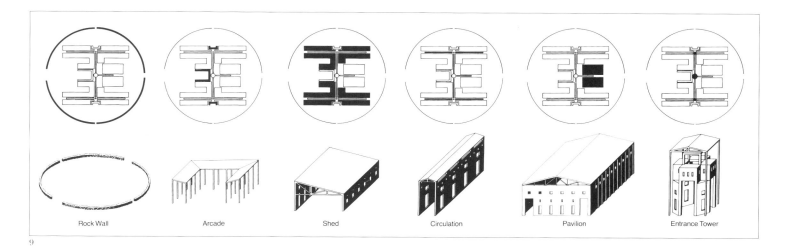

| Rock Wall | Arcade | Shed | Circulation | Pavilion | Entrance Tower |

9

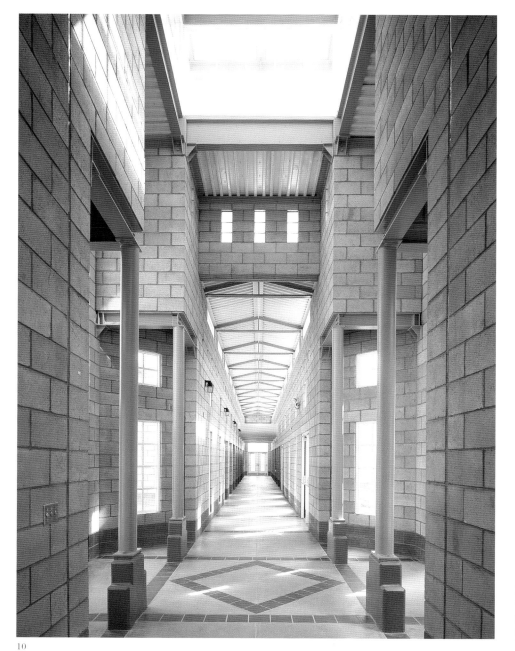

above define major circulation; translucent fiberglass roofs and canvas awnings define and shade exterior walkways and plazas. The shared, public elements are at the center of the axial composition.

The architectural language is an abstraction of the region's residential and agrarian architecture of simply detailed, masonry bearing walls, exposed steel construction and sloped metal roofs. The forms are monumental in shape but are reduced in scale to adjust to the size of the child.

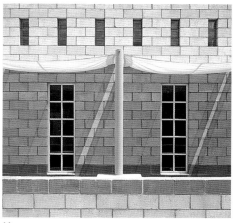

10

11

Troy High School

Design/Completion 1989/1992
Troy, Michigan
Troy Public Schools
300,000 square feet
Steel structure
Brick, aluminum-framed windows

The design for this 2,100-student high school responds to the school's natural site by weaving together interior and exterior spaces, not unlike Eliel Saarinen's Cranbrook Academy of Art in nearby Bloomfield Hills. Here, parallel bars of classrooms, connected by a perpendicular circulation spine, extend toward the wooded western edge of the site. This edge completes the enclosure of a series of outdoor rooms that become integral to the school environment. The classroom bars are a repetitive datum that contrasts with the sculptural, object-pavilions of the shared spaces of the school: the library, cafeteria, auditorium, gymnasium, and pool. The 750-seat auditorium and the athletic facilities are located at the periphery of the project, to enable separate community access after hours. A stair tower with vertically extended planar walls marks the main entrance to the south. It is a vertical marker in contrast to the horizontal emphasis of the whole.

1

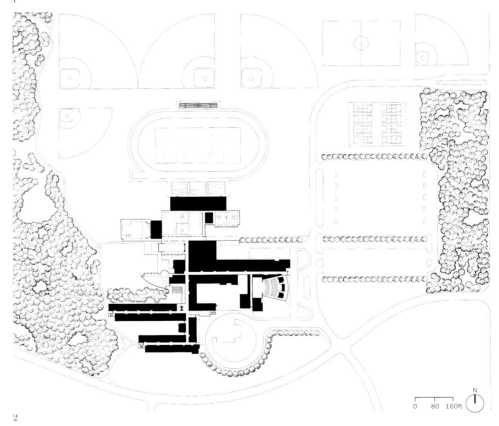

2

1 Overall view from southeast
2 Site plan
3 Section looking east
4 Main entry

18

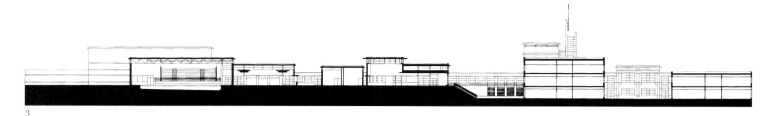

3

4

5

6

5   Exterior of library
6   View looking towards library from dining patio
7   Entry level plan
8   Stair lobby
9   Entry lobby

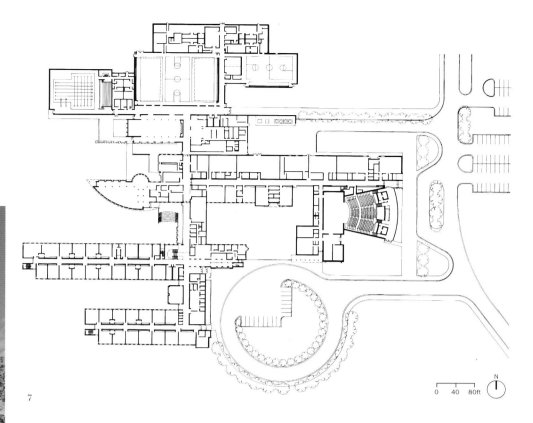

7

8

9

Perry Community Education Village

Design/Completion 1990/1995
Perry, Ohio
Perry Local School District
High school 210,000 square feet; middle school, 150,000 square feet;
elementary school, 100,000 square feet; fitness center, 180,000 square feet
Steel structure
Brick, aluminum and glass

The design of the Perry school, built for 4,500 students, further explores the organizing principles used in the Troy High School. A creek with mature stands of trees along its banks bisects the site: this setting suggested the creation of two campuses connected by an enclosed bridge. The west campus consists of the high school and community fitness center, while the east campus houses the middle and elementary schools. Each campus functions independently, with its own classrooms, laboratories, library, and arts facilities. Each has its own entrance plaza marked by tower, and vertical elements terminate each end of the connecting walkway.

Continued

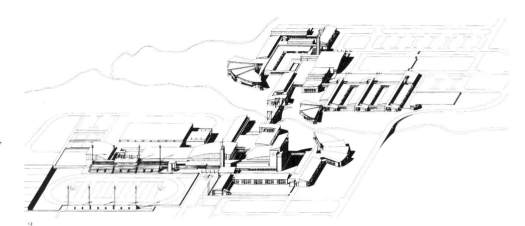

2

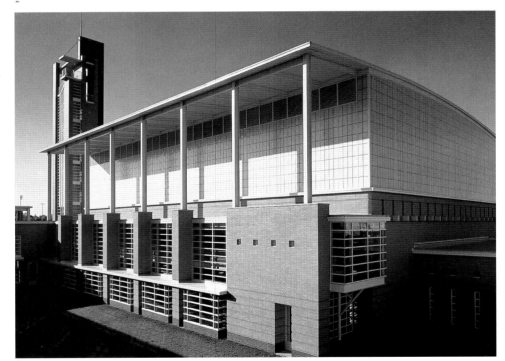

3

1 Classroom wing
2 Axonometric
3 Exterior view of gym
4 Entry view from west
5 Repeatable forms
6 Administration lobby

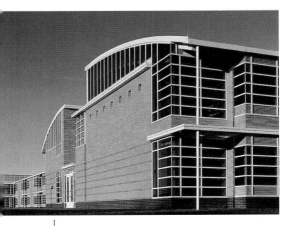

1

4

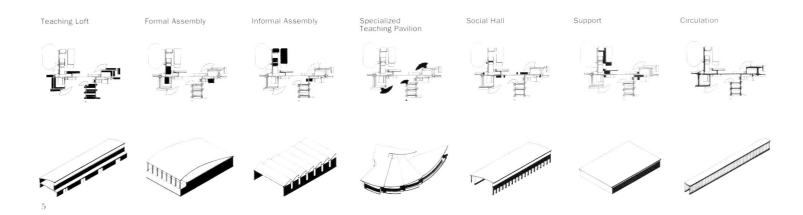

Teaching Loft   Formal Assembly   Informal Assembly   Specialized
Teaching Pavilion   Social Hall   Support   Circulation

5

6

7 Entry to performing arts and visual arts wing
8 View of academic classrooms with theatre and
  gyms in background

As with Troy High School, the classroom bars form the datum against which play the curved roofs of the assembly and fitness spaces, and the fan-shaped elements containing each school's library, and music and art departments. These more sculptural elements mediate between the orthogonal grid of the school and the irregular wooded edge along the creek. A series of formal types related to specific functions is used repetitively and is adapted to the specifics of the site in order to organize a complex program into discrete parts that are also understandable as a rich whole.

9

10

9   Theatre lobby perspective
10   Typical classroom
11   Interior administrative lobby
Opposite:
    Dining

11

26

North Fort Myers High School

Design/Completion 1992/1995
Fort Myers, Florida
Lee County School Board
226,000 square feet
Concrete and steel structure
Brick, aluminum/glass windows

The design of this 1,600-student high school uses simple geometries to integrate three existing buildings into a new whole that has a distinct sense of place. Two new classroom buildings, a single-loaded, linear bar, and a circle, link the existing auditorium, gymnasium, and renovated classroom buildings and their new additions. Placed within the circular classroom courtyard, the new media center is literally at the heart of the campus. Its triangular form is echoed by an expressive angled roof, and its geometry extends through the circle to link the gymnasium and newly renovated cafeteria/specialized classroom building.

Exterior rooms and connective spaces, such as exterior classroom corridors, covered walkways, terraces, and canopied entryways, take advantage of the gentle climate of southwest Florida. The landscape design represents different ecological environments in support of the environmental studies program.

1

2

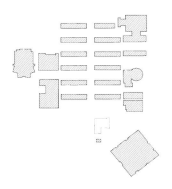

Existing Condition

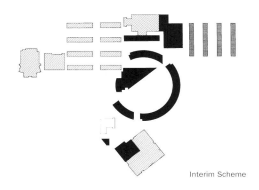

Interim Scheme

Final Scheme

3

Existing classrooms
Temporary Classrooms
New classrooms

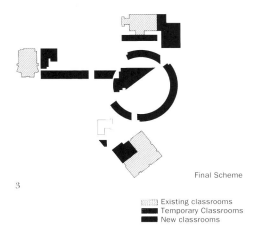

1   Library exterior
2   Courtyard view
3   Phasing diagrams
4   Bus entry
5   Second floor corridor

6

7

8

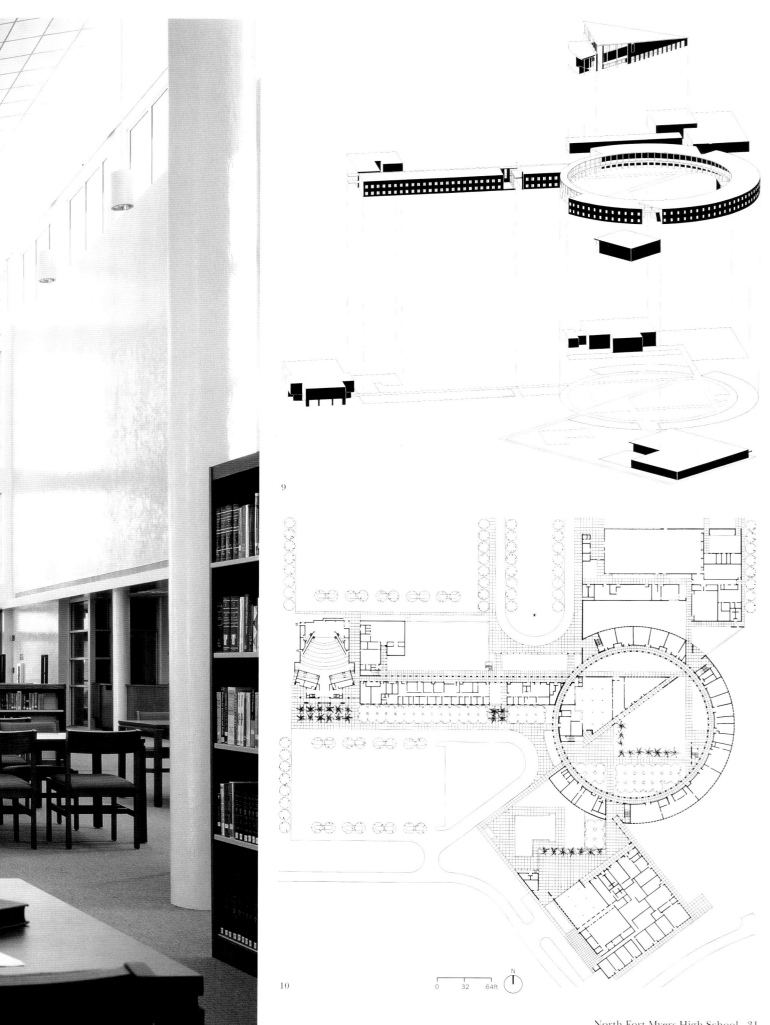

9

10

0 32 64ft

N

Chelsea High School

Design/Completion 1993/1996
Chelsea, Massachusetts
Chelsea School District
155,000 square feet
Steel structure
Brick, aluminum and glass curtainwall

This urban school is by necessity compact and vertically organized; it establishes itself at the southern edge of the site in order to make connections to its context, and to provide space for the playing fields. The school is divided into four interdisciplinary and autonomous "houses," each of which has a specific occupational and educational emphasis which reinforces the link between education and vocation. This internal organization is clearly articulated in the design, with each house occupying a 4-story, rowhouse-like unit and having its own staircase and street entrance on the south. These stairs help to modulate the south elevation, and to express the four distinct units within. Two community entrances from the east and west lead to a multi-level interior street which connects the shared spaces of the school—auditorium, library, music rooms, and gymnasium to the north—with the classroom houses and their individual dining spaces to the south. The skylit street brings natural light to interior classrooms. An open stair to the north leads to an upper-level, clerestoried library that overlooks the playing fields.

1

0   120 240ft

2

3

32

1 Site plan
2 View from south
3 Academy entry
4 North entry at library

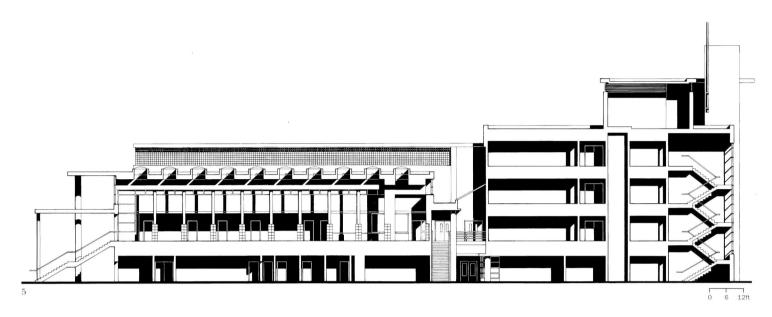

5

0　6　12ft

6

0　12　24ft

7

5　Section
6　First floor plan
7　Spine looking west
8　Library

8

International School Beijing–Shunyi

Design/ Completion 1995/2001
Beijing, People's Republic of China
International School Beijing–Shunyi
630,000 square feet
Concrete frame, pre-stressed, two-way slab for long span structures
Curtainwall, tile on masonry cavity wall, aluminum panel

Located northeast of the city of Beijing, the new campus for the International School of Beijing will consist of elementary, middle, and high schools for 2,600 students, as well as gardens, sports fields, a stadium, parking, and apartment housing for faculty members. The architecture is modern, yet makes reference to its cultural context through elements common to both Western Modernism and traditional Chinese architecture. The formal organizational element adopted from Chinese architecture is the private interior courtyard. Other formal devices include axial symmetry, with movement off axes or along edges, and layering the transition between interior and exterior spaces with loggias and screens. An architectural vocabulary of spatial framing is rigorously orthogonal, as in traditional Chinese architecture, and creates interesting ambiguities between building and landscape. A language of wrappers, or solid planes which turn two corners, creates complex spaces through simple moves.

Continued

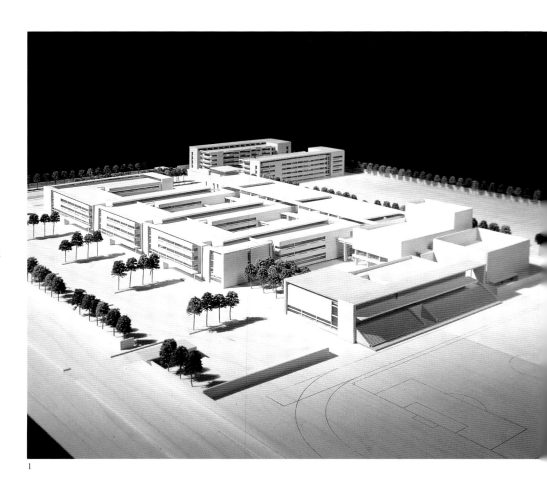

1

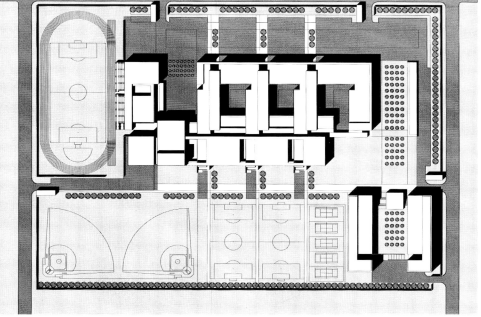

1   Model view from northwest
2   Site plan
3   Section through theatre and main entry court
4   Model view from north

2

0   20   40ft   N

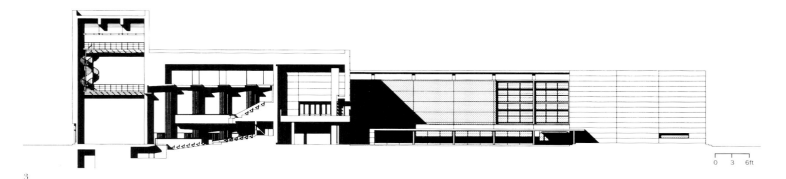

3

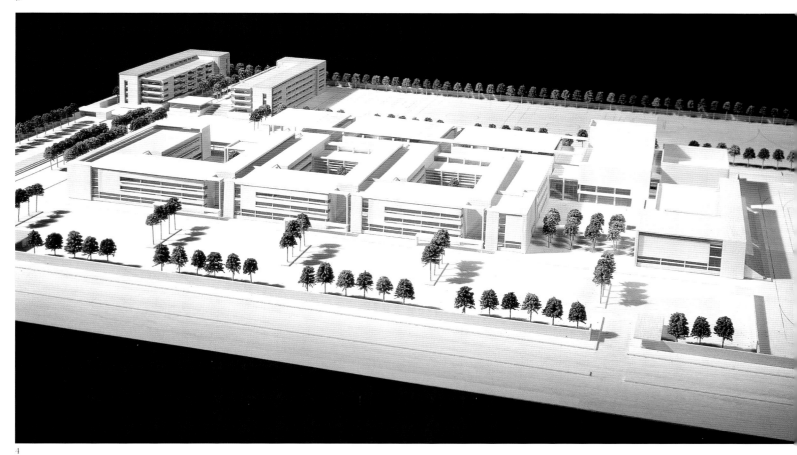

4

The campus is located in a field, framed by a site wall and regulated by an orthogonal grid of pathways. All three schools are condensed into one compound building made up of two opposing Ls that separate classrooms from the large shared functions of theater, cafeterias, gymnasiums, and swimming pool. An east–west public spine links the two bar buildings and their functions. Administrative offices bridge across the two Ls, forming four courtyards which provide identity to each of the three schools and the public entrance. Within each courtyard, libraries and group rooms act as focal points. The overlapping of the school's opposing-L and courtyard partis creates a spatial layering, with informal gathering spaces located at the points of overlap. Each school is organized around a procession through its courtyard, marked by brightly-colored screen walls. The public procession is more formal, and begins with the public court offering entry to public spaces.

The faculty housing—located in the southeast corner of the site—is divided into two symmetrical, 4-story buildings, forming a courtyard that visually extends the garden to the east of the school. A community pavilion provides a focal point for the school's garden, and marks the entry to the housing area's raised courtyard. As in traditional Chinese planning, the façades on the courtyard are open and delicate, while the façades on the exterior are more solid, relating to the school buildings.

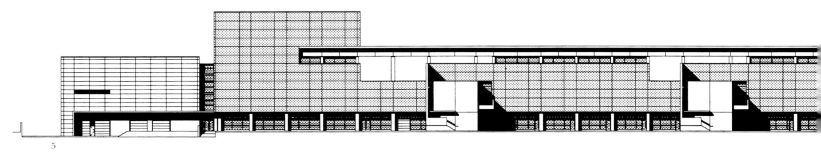

5

6

7

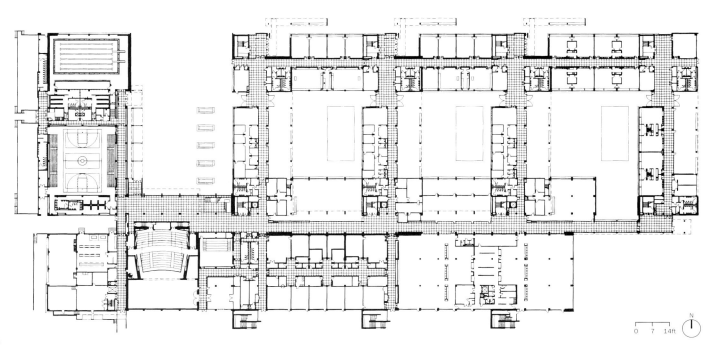

8

0   7   14ft   N

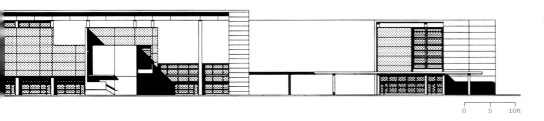

0 5 10ft

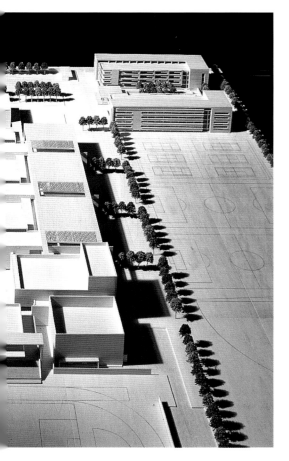

9

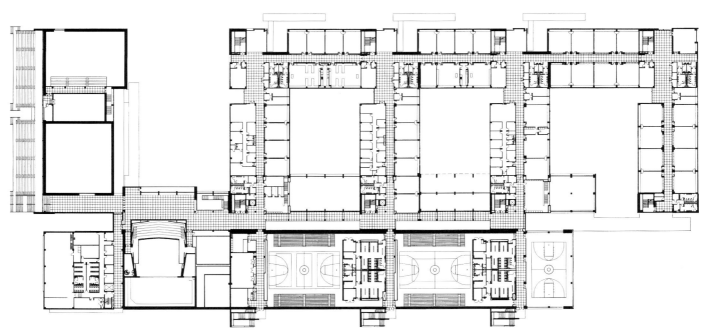

10

International School of Manila

Design/Completion 1996/2000
Manila, Philippines
International School of Manila
55,000 square meters
Concrete with structural steel
Stucco, exposed concrete and native stone, aluminum windows
and sun shades, curtainwall, Philippine mahogany railings

The new facilities for the International School of Manila, which is currently housed in various older buildings in downtown Manila, is being constructed in the Fort Bonifacio development area, on the outskirts of the city. The new facility will house 3,000 students from kindergarten level through to high school, and will provide recreational facilities and adult education to the community.

The two main bars of the building, one curved and one straight, interlock at the main public entrance, and provide a monumental image and focal point for the residential development in the area. The curve responds to an existing curved road, while the north–south bar overlooks the athletic fields. The shared public spaces, such as the pool, gymnasium, library, and cafeteria, occupy this north–south bar along the main entrance spine, while perpendicular classroom clusters and the arcing bar of classrooms enclose courtyard spaces that internally break down the scale of the school. The development of inner, cloistered courtyards was derived from Spanish Colonial architecture in the Philippines. Each school has its own entrance off the inner curved road, and each focuses inward on its own courtyard, which is punctuated by a "teacher tower" for faculty. The courtyard spaces step down in height as the roof of the curved bar slopes down from five stories to two. Classrooms for the youngest children are in the lower portion of the building, farthest from the main public entry.

1

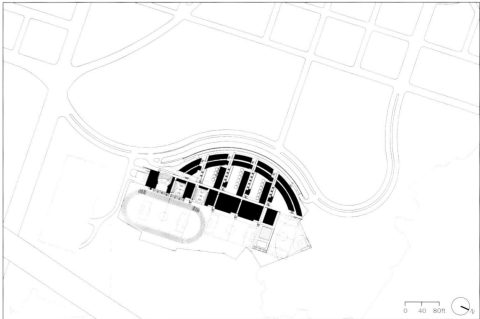

2

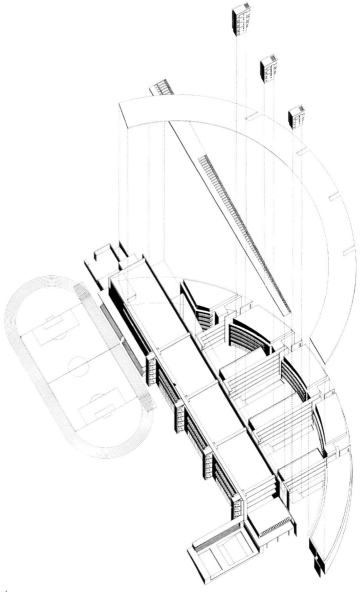

3

4

1   Model view from north
2   Site plan
3   Aerial view of model
4   Exploded axonometric

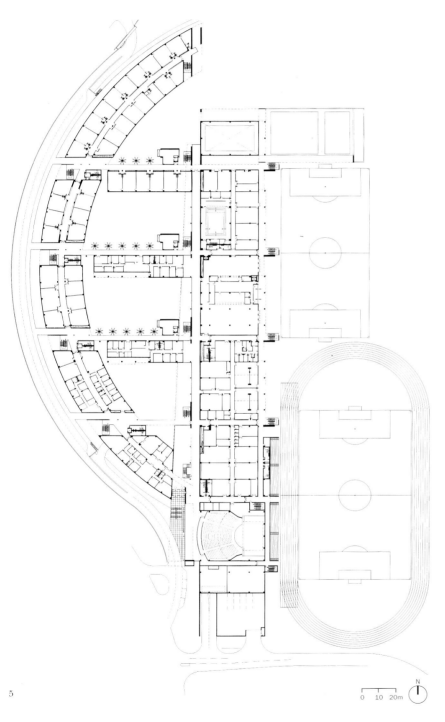

5

5 First floor plan
6 Model view from south
7 Entry perspective
8 Courtyard perspective

6

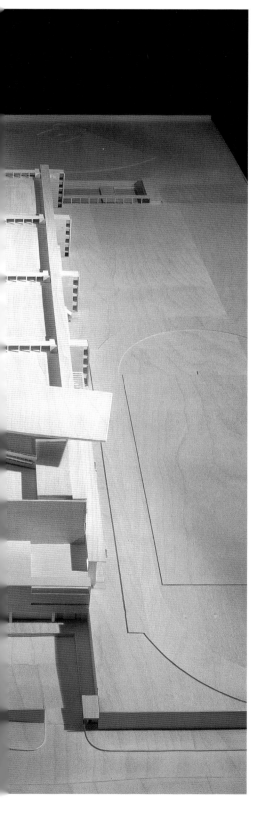

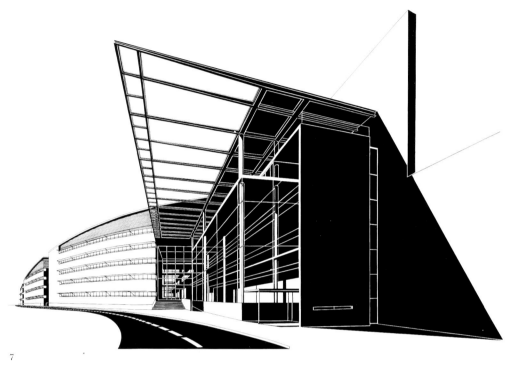

7

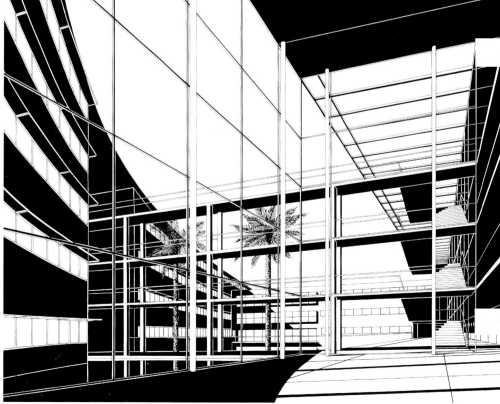

8

Fearn Elementary School

Design/Completion 1999/2001
North Aurora, Illinois
West Aurora School District
58,000 square feet
Slab on grade, steel frame construction
Brick faced perimeter walls

The design of this new kindergarten to grade 5 elementary school looks to the Crow Island School, designed by Perkins Wheeler and Will in collaboration with Eliel and Eero Saarinen, as a precedent, but analyses and transforms elements of that design. The L-shaped classroom is adopted as the basic building block, but classrooms have been grouped into clusters of four, resulting in "suites" of rooms centered around shared resource areas.

The gently arcing main corridor is a public, indoor street with continuous clerestory lighting. The extended trajectory of this arc becomes a path linking the new school to the recently completed middle school, located across the fields to the southeast. In contrast to the arc of classrooms, the kindergarten, teaching laboratory and administrative wing, and the multi-purpose hall which faces them, are simple rectilinear forms. An intermediate transition zone resulting from these contrasting geometries becomes a series of cul-de-sacs; the activities there become highly visible "storefront" operations along the street.

Sitting on the edge of the open prairie, in a fast-growing western suburb of Chicago, the gestural quality of the curve mediates between the rectilinear traces of farm fields and the curving cul-de-sacs of the adjacent housing developments. The composition of intimate classroom clusters and curving street; the big gesture of the arc versus the intimate patios and terraces at front and back of the school; and the horizontal expression of mullions and brick all help to establish a sense of sheltered space, and create a specific sense of place within an instantly created and rapidly growing neighborhood.

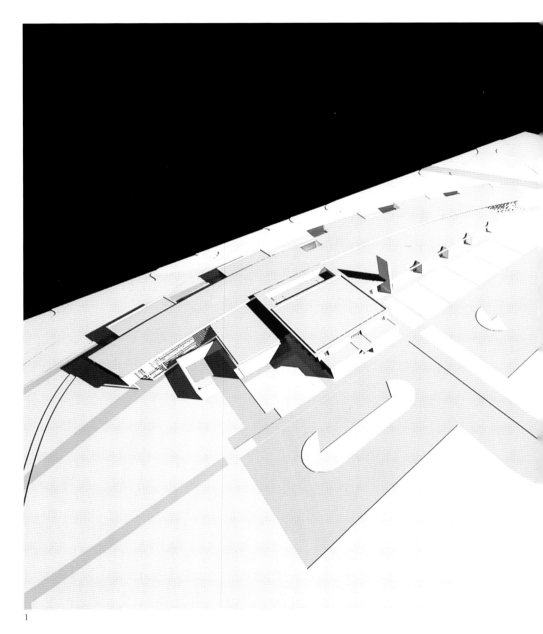

1

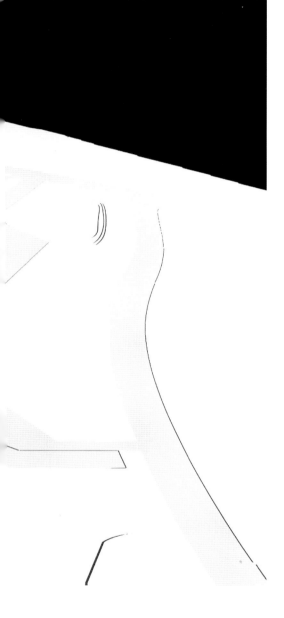

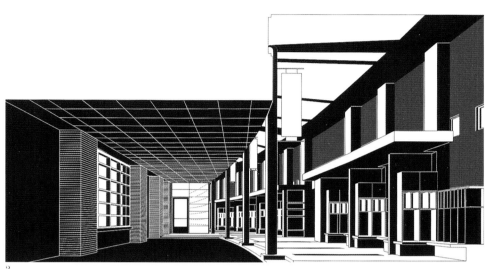

2

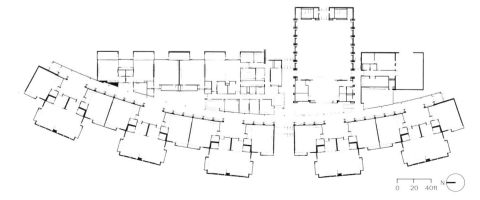

3

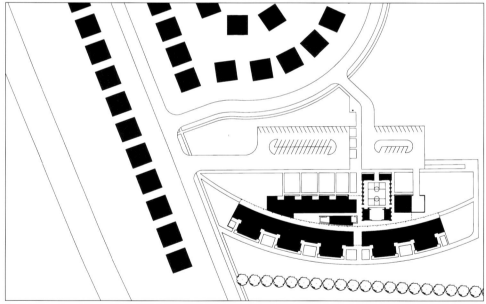

1   Aerial view
2   Interior perspective
3   Site plan
4   Floor plan

4

Charter School

Design/Completion 1999/
Chicago, Illinois
Prologue
100,000 square feet
Concrete
Concrete, brick, glass

This 100,000-squar- foot charter school, designed to house 900 elementary school students, is located in a planned redevelopment zone in the Englewood neighborhood of Chicago's south side. An elevated transit line bisects the site. The smaller portion of the site to the north of the tracks faces a commercial street, while the larger lot to the south fronts a residential area. The school is sited on the latter, with the smaller parcel reserved for parking and future commercial development. The school is seen as an urban element which, along with other adjacent developments, could catalyze the redevelopment of this area of Englewood.

The building's L-shaped organization anchors it to the dominant urban element on the site—the elevated tracks—and encloses a private, walled outdoor-play space. The public components of the school program, such as the gymnasium, cafeteria, library, and administrative offices are located in a block adjacent and parallel to the elevated tracks. The classrooms form a rectilinear block perpendicular to the public block, and a plaza at the corner links the two. The massing of the public block responds to the commercial buildings to the north, and the massing of the classroom block responds to the residential neighborhood which it faces to the south.

The gymnasium buffers the remainder of the school from the noise of the trains, and is also a community room which can be opened up to the public plaza by means of pivoting doors. This outdoor room, open but roofed, is the actual entry to the school, as well as a threshold space connecting the building with its community. The classroom block contains the three academies of the school—one per floor—each of which is broken down into four houses composed of three classrooms. This organization creates smaller social units that provide students with a sense of place within the school. Classrooms, library, and cafeteria are oriented toward the walled courtyard space.

Continued

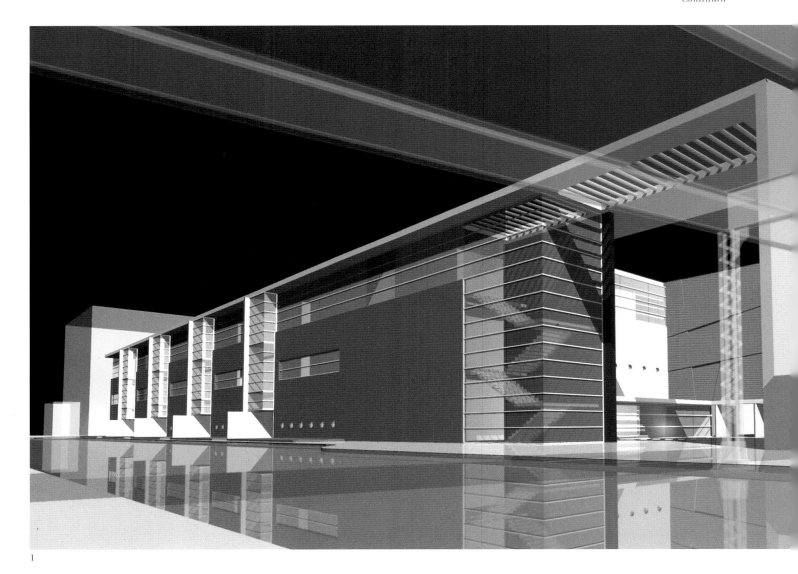

1

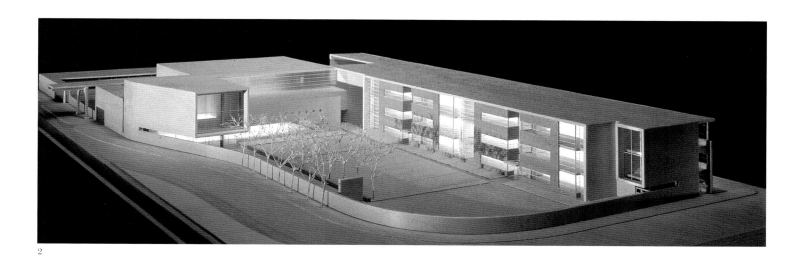

2

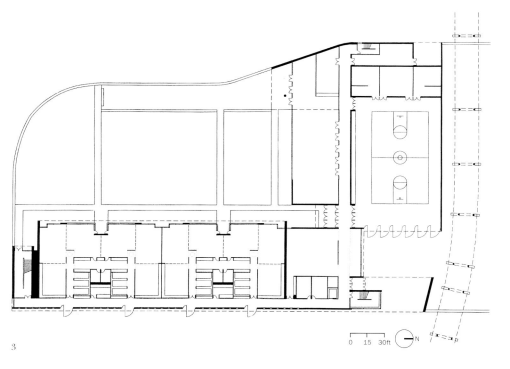

3

1   View from northeast
2   Model view from southwest
3   Ground floor plan

The building's architectural expression reinforces the public and private organizational concept, by articulating programmatic differences and linking the disparate parts into one whole. A precast-concrete envelope distinguishes the public/community components from the classroom spaces clad in brick. Concrete is also employed as a wrapper that ties together the public and private elements of the school; it moves from the wall of the courtyard to the roof of the classrooms, and is finally expressed as the precast trellis over the entry plaza. This abstract concrete plane also provides an overall framework under which the four brick house elements are vertically articulated.

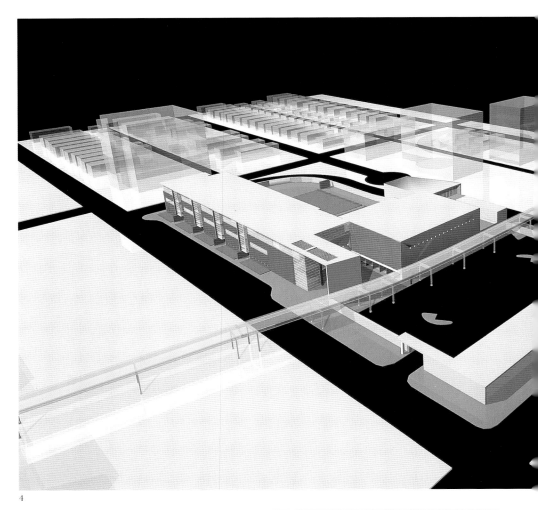

4

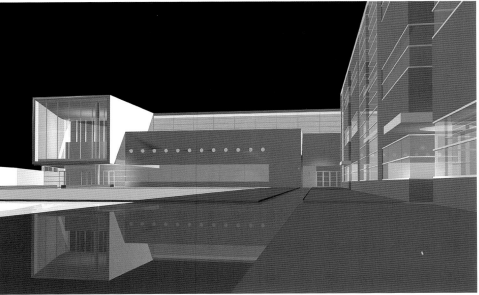

5

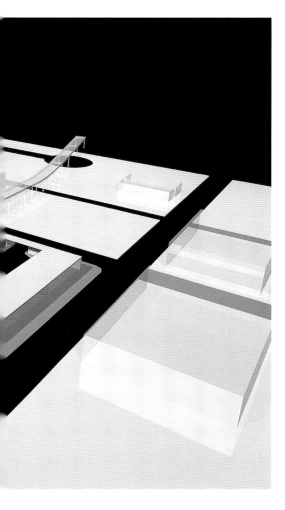

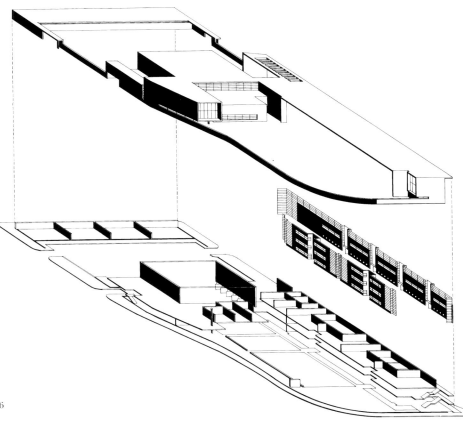

6

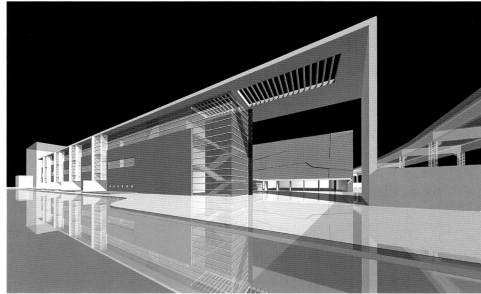

4   View from northeast
5   Outdoor playspace, looking north
6   Exploded axonometric
7   View looking through entry

7

Higher Education

Temple Hoyne Buell Hall
University of Illinois Urbana-Champaign

Design/Completion 1990/1995
Champaign, Illinois
University of Illinois, Urbana-Champaign/ Capital Development Board
109,000 square feet
Structural steel and concrete
Brick, aluminum curtainwall

Temple Hoyne Buell Hall houses the graduate schools of Architecture, Landscape Architecture, and Urban Planning of the University of Illinois. The design responds to two primary concerns. Firstly, that the building's placement and form should formally interpret the nature of its position at the intersection of the campus's two major axes: the north–south axis of the University quadrangle, planned by C.H. Blackall in 1905, and the military axis suggested by architect Charles Platt in 1922. Secondly, that the building's organization and expression should encourage interdisciplinary teaching between the three schools, which were previously housed in separate buildings.

The resulting building is a link between the past and future of the University, a working example of the craft of architecture, and a physical representation of the integration of landscape, urban planning, and architecture. Four elements define a multi-level internal courtyard. The two rectilinear volumes housing the loft-like studio spaces and department offices define the intersection of the two campus axes. Their façade expression interprets the Georgian architecture of

Continued

1

2

3

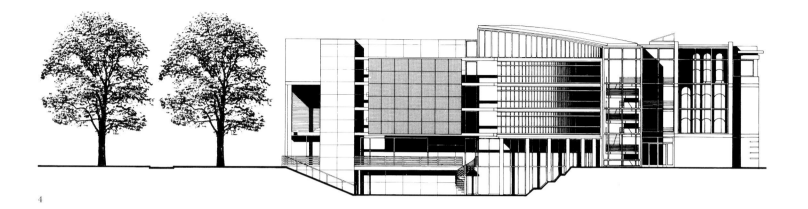

4

5

Temple Hoyne Buell Hall, University of Illinois Urbana-Champaign   53

many structures on campus, including the 1920s Architecture Building, and is rectilinear, contextual, and ordered. On the interior courtyard side, two lyrical, modern components are set against the masonry studio volumes, creating a stark contrast to the public face. One is a curvilinear bar of glass raised off the ground so that the courtyard space might penetrate into the interior. This building houses the faculty offices. The other is a 4-story media wall, projected off the wall of the north volume, and designed for indoor and outdoor audiovisual presentations. Together, the components of the buildings define a space that symbolizes the interdisciplinary aspirations of the three departments.

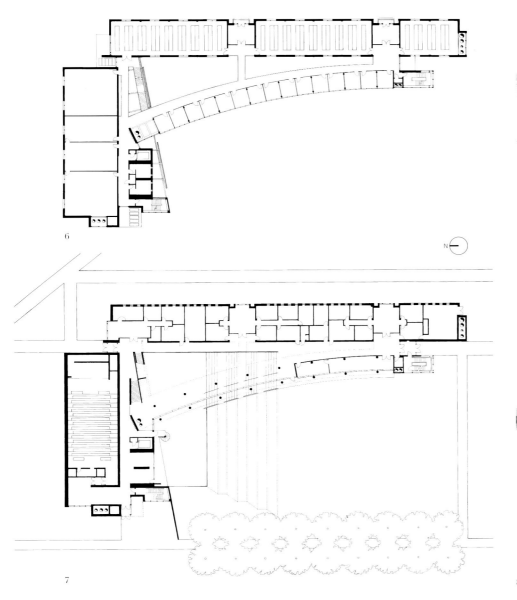

6

7

8

9

10

Monroe Community College

Design/ Completion 1990/1994
Rochester, New York
Monroe Community College
120,000 square feet new/ 50,000 square feet renovation
Concrete waffle slab
Brick-on-masonry cavity wall, aluminum panel, curtainwall

The new Fine Arts Building and the Instructional Resources (Science) Building were identified on the master plan developed by Perkins & Will for Monroe Community College's 300-acre campus. The focus of the master plan was to improve the internal circulation of the campus, to develop new buildings sympathetic to the existing campus, and to provide new classroom space.

The design solution inserts the two new buildings into the existing 1960s, E-shaped building campus, transforming it into a traditional quadrangle building and creating a new academic image for the campus. The new buildings enclose two separate courtyards and create new internal circulation. This circulation spine provides not only new points of entry, but also much needed student lounge space, and greatly facilitates circulation throughout the facility. The north wing atrium also provides gathering and performance space for the College's Little Theater, and is the front door of a new student art gallery. The south wing atrium is the major entry from the east.

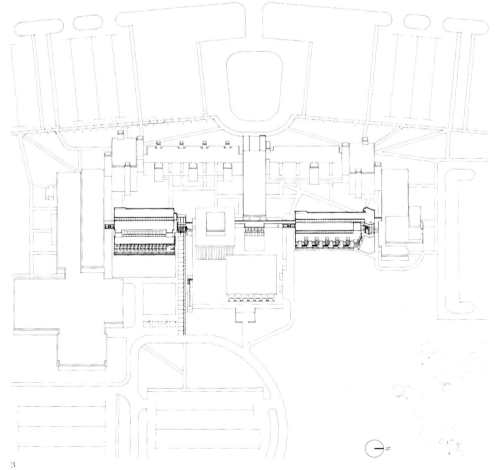

1

2

3

1 Instructional Resource Center, east elevation
2 Fine Arts west elevation
3 Site plan
4 Design sketch
5 Detail of art studio bay
6 Instructional Resource Center

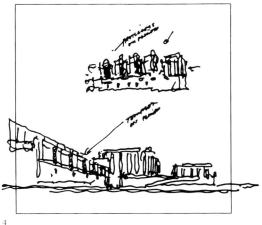

4

5

6

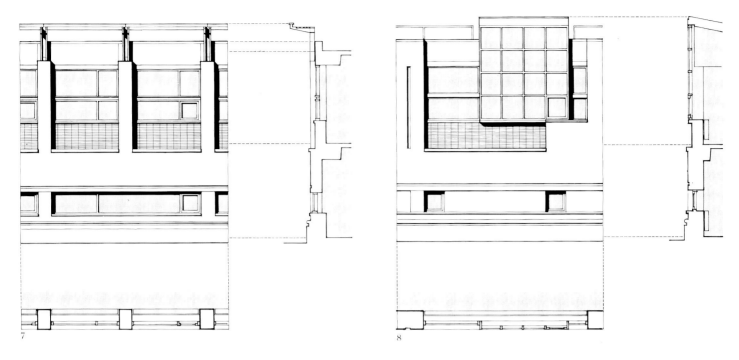

7

8

9

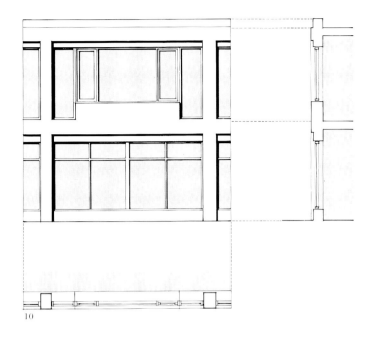

10

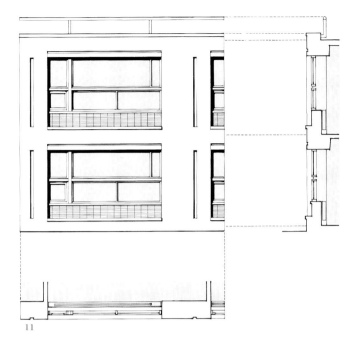

11

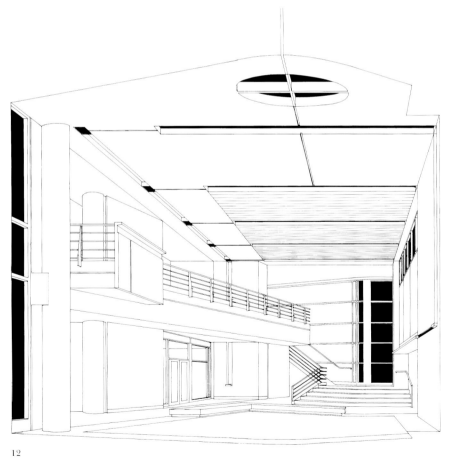

12

13

7   Instructional Resource Center bay
8   Art Studio bay
9   Fine Arts Building atrium lobby
10 Existing courtyard bay
11 Courtyard bay
12 Fine Arts Building, atrium perspective
13 Entry to Instructional Resource Center

Emory University, North Decatur Building

Design/Completion 1993/1994
Atlanta, Georgia
Emory University
120,000 square feet
Poured-in-place concrete structure
Stucco, green insulated glass, solid and striped spandrel
glass in painted white metal frame

Since the North Decatur Building is
the first building one encounters on the
northern edge of the campus, this project
provided the opportunity to create a major
gateway image for Emory University. The
broad sweep of the curved curtainwall,
with its articulated sunscreening devices,
creates a large-scale presence on this
prominent corner. The 4-story recess at
the entry reflects the wedge-shaped lobby
behind, which has a cascading stair
leading to a second-level bridge
connection to the adjacent building.

The project consolidates computer
operations facilities for Emory University,
Emory University Hospital, Crawford Long
Hospital, and The Emory Clinic. Included
in the facility are a data center equipment
area, office and support spaces, academic
spaces, training rooms, and an informatics
program—a research and development
computer operation for medical
professionals. The University's Math
and Computer Sciences Department and
Educational Studies Department are also
located in this facility, occupying two levels
and having academic offices, classrooms,
a large auditorium, and a variety of
computer labs.

1

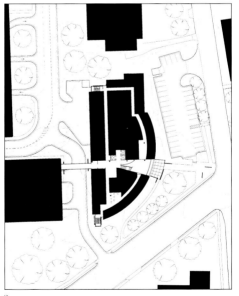

2

3

1   Campus elevation
2   Site plan
3&4   Exterior wall

4

Emory University, Cox Hall

Design/Completion 1992/1993
Atlanta, Georgia
Emory University
60,000 square feet
Poured-in-place concrete structure
Stucco, green insulated glass and solid spandrel glass in painted white metal frames, precast-concrete piers, painted metal louver sunscreens, poured-in-place terrazzo patio

The renovation and expansion of Cox Hall provides a new and inviting public image for this multi-purpose facility, which is centrally located on the Emory University campus. The facility includes food service, conference space, and academic space on two levels. The lower level houses the renovated kitchen, a new fast-food servery, and seating for 350. Seating for an additional 40 is accommodated on the exterior plaza, which opens off the dining room and fronts a main pedestrian corridor. The freestanding elevator/clock tower is a focal point for the plaza, and the main façade with its columns and sun shades provides scale and an active play of light and shadow. Between the tower and the building, a gracious exterior staircase leads to the upper level, which houses a new, 500-seat multi-purpose ballroom, smaller meeting rooms, and a catering kitchen.

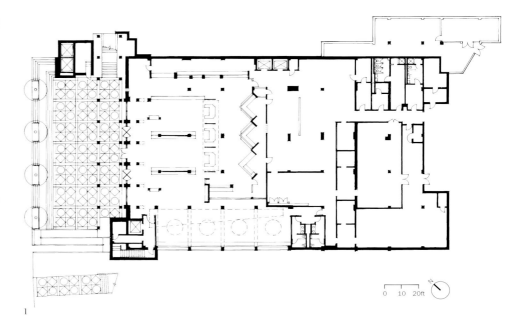

1

1   Ground floor plan
2   Patio

2

Fuqua School of Business, Student Center, Duke University

Design/Completion: 1998/2001
Durham, North Carolina
Duke University
90,000 square feet
Steel frame
Precast concrete and glass

Situated between and connecting the east and west wings of the Keller Center, the student center will become the functional and physical center of student life at the School of Business. A sawtooth roof provides natural light for the building's main spaces: the winter garden, dining room, and student lounge below. These light, glazed spaces also project outwards, with views toward the woods and connections to outdoor terraces. Other spaces include changing rooms with lockers and showers, a student communications center, and a computer lab and multimedia facility. On its west side, the student center connects to the existing west wing tower via a new administrative mini-tower.

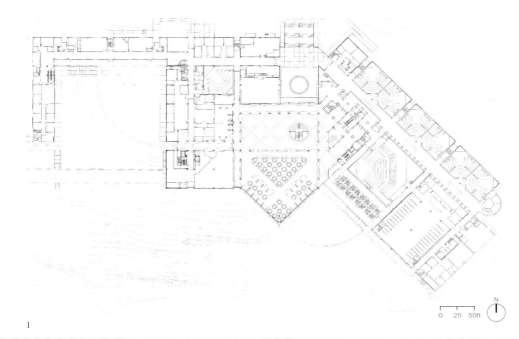

0   25   50ft

1

2

1   First floor plan
2   Interior

University of Miami, School of Communication

Design/Completion: 1996/2000
Coral Gables, Florida
University of Miami
50,000 square feet
Concrete structure
Precast concrete, block and stucco.

The School of Communication
consolidates facilities which had been
scattered across the campus for many
years. The new structure wraps around the
existing cablevision studios, creating a new
student commons in the resulting 3-story
courtyard. The stair tower marks the
corner, and the breezeway connecting to
the courtyard passes between the tower
and an arcade, which frames and redefines
the southern entrance to the campus. The
building contains writing laboratories, film
studios, photography labs and animation
suites, and through its design represents
the union of technology and campus
tradition.

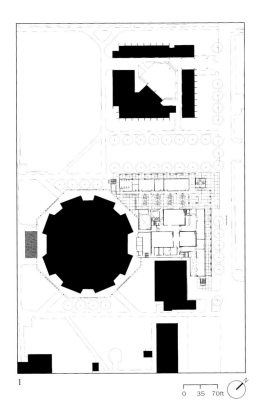

1

0   35   70ft

2

1   Site plan
2   Model view from north
3   Aerial view
4   View to courtyard from south

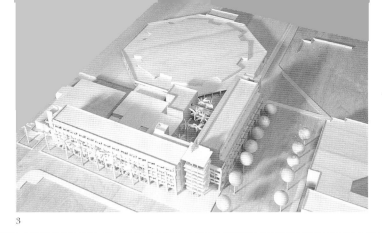

3

4

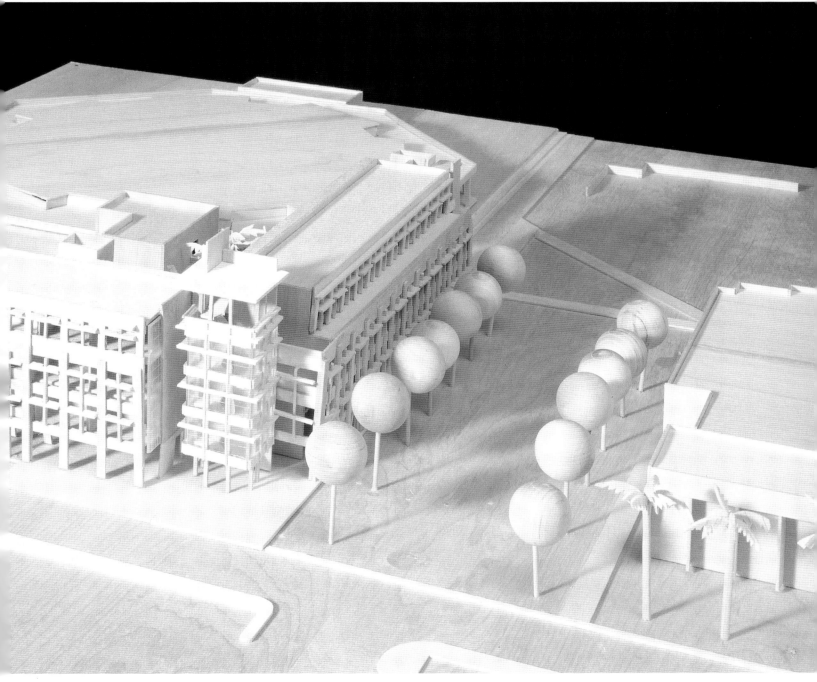

University of Chicago
Graduate School of Business Competition

Design/Completion 1999
Chicago, Illinois
University of Chicago
285,000 square feet
Steel structure
Limestone, aluminum and glass curtainwall, kalwall

The challenge of the University of Chicago Graduate School of Business design was to acknowledge the historic tradition and spatial quality of the University of Chicago campus, while creating a new image for the School of Business. Designed as a series of quadrangles by Henry Ives Cobb in the 1890s, the campus is predominantly Gothic in character, and is constructed of limestone. The strategy adopted was to create a new quadrangle enclosed on three sides by the three components of the building program: the center for student life, the academic center, and the faculty-administrative center. Noyes Hall, an existing Gothic building, completes the south side of the quadrangle and sets up an axis with the central function space of the business school, the physical and symbolic link between the three pavilions.

Not only does the pavilion approach respond to the scale of the existing campus and the desire on the part of the business school to have three discrete functional components, but it also allows the pavilions to respond locally to the varied scale and expression of the immediate context. The student life pavilion and main entrance face the center of the campus to the west, and relate to the east–west axis of Rockefeller Chapel across the street. This pavilion's larger-scale, glazed openings complement the powerful scale of the chapel. The classroom pavilion, to the north, is lower and more horizontal, responding to Frank Lloyd Wright's Robie House and other residences to the north. Four-story vertical wings in the faculty pavilion recall the repetitive vertical articulation of the University Lab School. The central quadrangle and use of limestone throughout unite the whole.

Throughout the building, gathering spaces point to the interdependence of the program components, and encourage informal interaction as well as structured learning. The central function space, 2-story faculty lounges, lobbies and stairs create common meeting grounds for the academic community.

1

2

3

4

5

6   Interior atrium
7   First floor plan, site plan

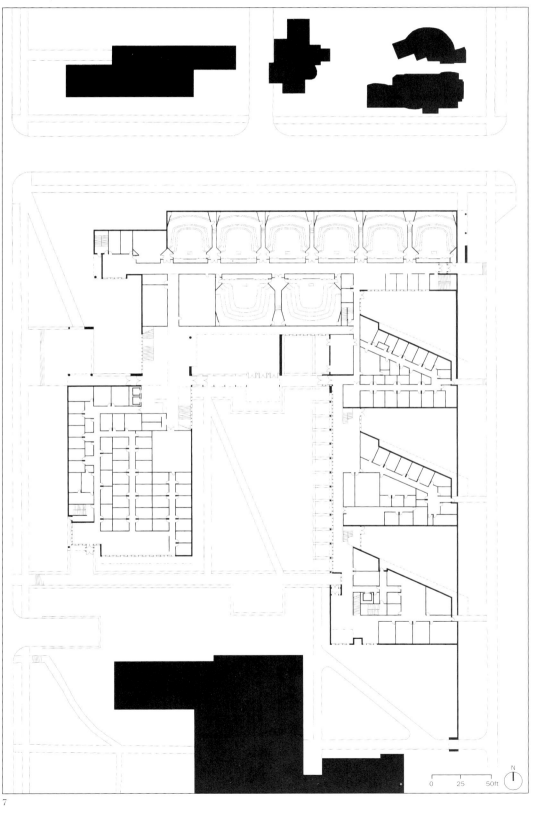

7

UCSD School of Medicine, Neighborhood Planning Study

Design/Completion 1999/2000
San Diego, California
University of California, San Diego
Two sites were studied—a developed western site (54 acres),
and an undeveloped eastern site (17 acres).

The School of Medicine neighborhood, located at the southern edge of UCSD's western campus, is comprised of teaching and research facilities ranging in height from one to five stories. The purpose of this planning study was to explore expansion and development potential while maintaining and strengthening the open, green spaces that give the campus its character. A major function of the study was to provide planning and urban design

guidelines to establish a plant palette for landscaped spaces; to identify development parcels; to define the overall massing of subsequent buildings; to define the potential density of site development; and to provide general direction for the parallel expansion of infrastructure. Reinforcement of the pedestrian access and strengthening the east–west connections were important considerations.

A new academic mall will serve as the focal point for new facilities within the expanded neighborhood, to the south. The expansion program includes a new School of Pharmacy, several 2–4-story teaching facilities, a satellite central plant, research facilities along the perimeter of the site, and a residential precinct at its southern point. Total build-out includes approximately 1.2 million square feet of new program space and 2,200 additional parking spaces.

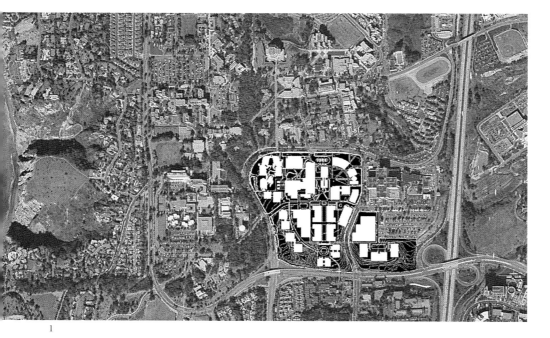

1

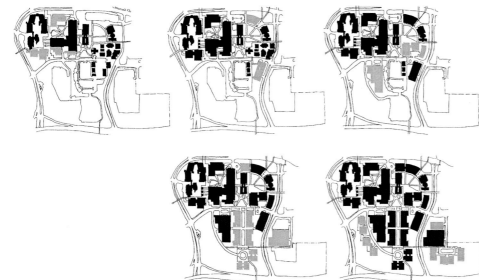

2

1 Site plan
2 Phasing diagrams

Miami Dade Community College, Aviation Training Center

Design/Completion 1999/2001
Homestead, Florida
Miami Dade County Public Schools
34,000 square feet
Concrete
Concrete, metal, glass, stainless steel panel

The new School of Aviation at Miami Dade Community College will house the latest in avionics technology, including three simulator labs, a tower room, pilot briefing rooms, computer classrooms, and conference rooms. The building will also house general campus services such as the campus bookstore, main cafeteria, and multi-purpose room.

The final structure planned for the campus, the aviation school, completes the triangular quadrangle and becomes its main entrance, facing US Route 1. The building forms an open gate to the quadrangle, with entry passing under the multi-purpose room; opaque glass surfaces transform this room into a lantern to the community. The 67-foot-high control tower room anchors the corner of the site. At the ground floor are the general campus services and an arcade that connects to existing building arcades. An exterior stair leads to the second floor lobby, which weaves the programmatic elements of the aviation school into a common space. Connections to adjacent buildings are also made at the second floor. Exposed concrete, metal panels, and laminated glass are the predominant materials, allowing the control tower, clad in stainless steel panels, to become the pivot point at the corner. Innovative spaces, materials and spatial sequencing create a dynamic structure, symbolic of flight, and appropriate to the history and future of aviation in South Florida.

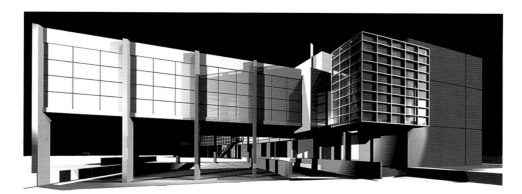

1

2

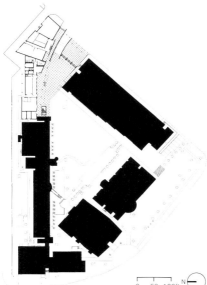

1   Entry from east
2   Arcade and stair to second floor lobby
3   Ground floor, site plan

3

0   50 100ft   N

George Mason University

Design/Completion: 1999/2002
Prince William County, Virginia
George Mason University
100,000 square feet
Steel structure
Glass curtainwall, metal, brick

This classroom building is for the Prince William Campus, the third George Mason University campus in northern Virginia. The 2- and 3-story building is the fourth building to be erected on this new campus, and it will house classrooms, lecture halls, teaching laboratories, offices, and a television studio. The building is located on axis with a new entry road and, with the existing buildings, will begin to form a new quadrangle.

The building's massing expresses its programmatic functions: a 2-story, square volume houses offices, and classrooms make up the 3-story linear volume. The classroom volume defines both the edge of the campus and the new quadrangle. The classroom bar is further broken down into two volumes around a 3-story transparent atrium which will become the interactive center and vertical binding element of the building. A 3-story cascading stair unites a series of breakout spaces and lounges on each level into a continuous social space. A wrapping roof plane unifies the volumes of the composition into a single urban campus element.

1   Entry view
Opposite:
    Atrium

1

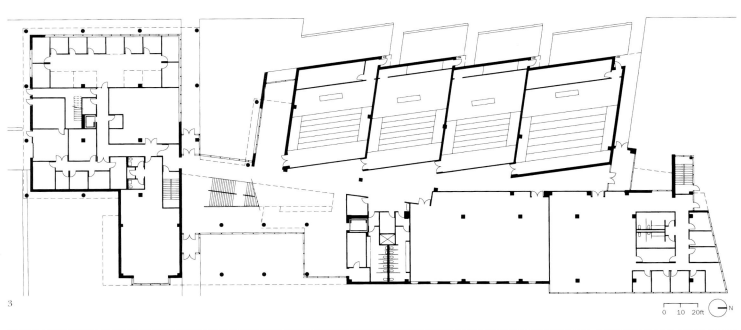

3

0 10 20ft N

4

3 Ground floor plan
4 Second level
5 Second floor plan
6 View from top of stair

5

6

Laboratories

Tarry Research and Education Building, Northwestern University

Design/Completion 1986/1990
Chicago, Illinois
Northwestern University
272,000 square feet
Steel structure
Limestone cladding, aluminum window and curtain wall systems

The challenge of the Tarry Research & Education Building design was twofold: to express the technical nature of a modern research laboratory while remaining sympathetic to the collegiate Gothic buildings of Northwestern's downtown campus, and to develop modern laboratory facilities within the limitations of connecting to an existing 1920s building. The constricted site is the southwest corner of a block with buildings that had been constructed at various times from the 1920s through to the 1960s for Northwestern University School of Medicine.

The laboratory layout was generated in part by the low, floor-to-floor height, dictated by the need to connect onto older buildings to the north and east. Modular laboratory spaces cluster around vertical chases frequently spaced to minimize the horizontal ceiling ducts. Faculty office and support spaces wrap the perimeter of the typical laboratory floor. Teaching labs occupy the lower floors, with flexible research labs located above. A faculty

Continued

1

80

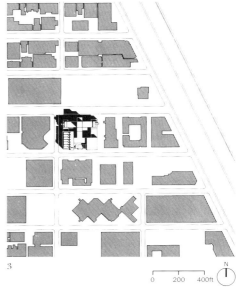

1 View from southwest
2 Entrance and connection between old and new
3 Site plan
4 Aerial view from southwest

5

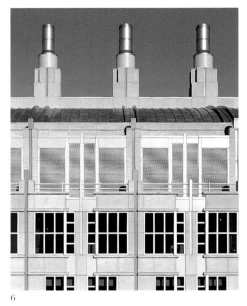

6

club occupies the south end of the top floor of the building. The new entrance lobby unifies circulation between new and existing buildings.

Limestone cladding and vertical window proportions are consistent with—but do not replicate—the Gothic structures; the materials and form mediate between context and a modern expression. The elevator core is expressed in a way which suggests an abstraction of the Gothic tower, and the vertical exhaust ducts on the roof are technological elements transformed into modern spires.

7

5   Top of building
6   Roof detail
7   Lobby inside entrance
8   Typical laboratory floor plan
9   Ground floor plan

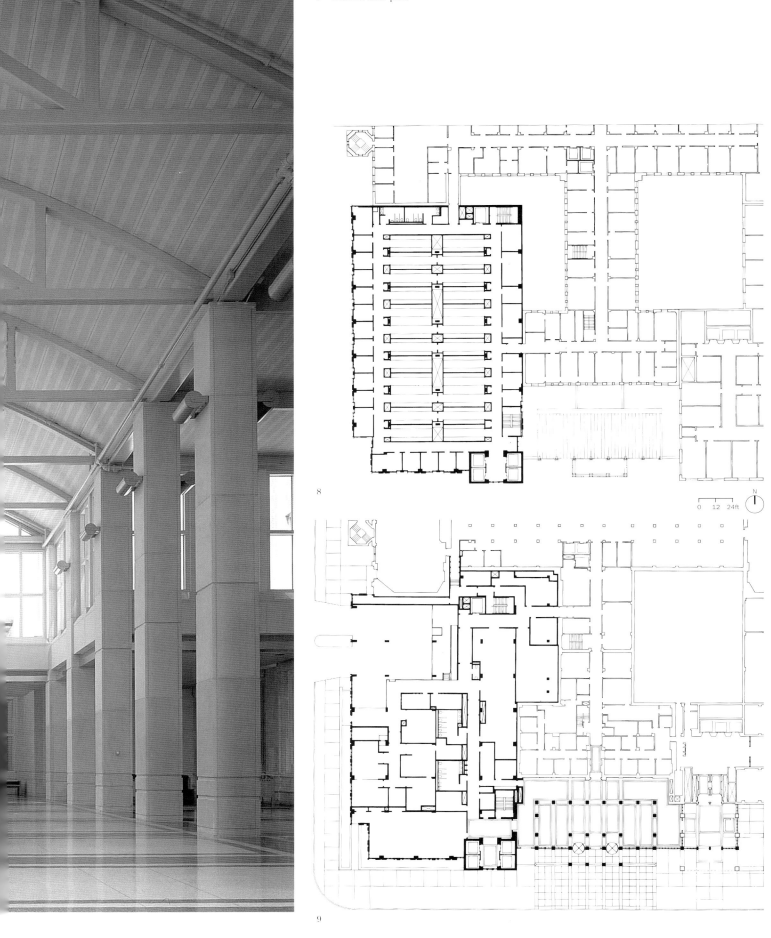

8

0   12   24ft   N

9

Vernal G. Riffe, Jr. Building, Ohio State University

Design/Completion 1990/1994
Columbus, Ohio
The Ohio State University
128,000 square feet
Concrete structure
Brick, metal panel and glass

By joining two existing laboratory
buildings, this biological sciences research
building transforms a poorly defined area
of medical and research buildings into a
gateway which defines the western edge
of The Ohio State University campus.
The two 1970s buildings, the College
of Biological Sciences and Parks Hall,
became part of a larger whole that creates
a presence as seen from across the athletic
fields to the north. The articulated
components express the functions within,
and engage the campus. The research
block, with its horizontal bands of metal
and glass, hovers above the two-story base
of shared facilities. The first floor of this
base defines the edge of the pedestrian
walkway, while the curved prow of the
second-floor library reading room engages
the path to the dormitories and follows the
curve of the fields. Four stacks demarcate
the building's function, and a vertical
tower of stacked discussion areas anchors
the composition.

Continued

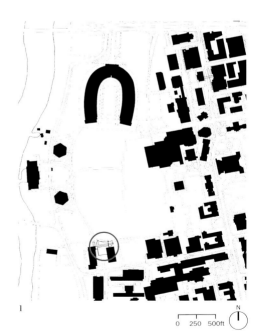

1

0   250   500ft   N

2

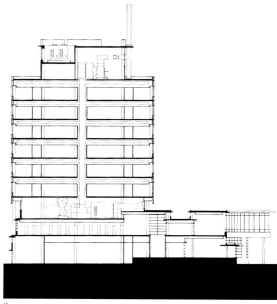

3

1　Site plan
2　View from northwest
3　Section

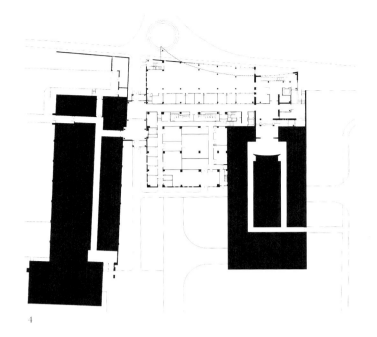

4

5

6

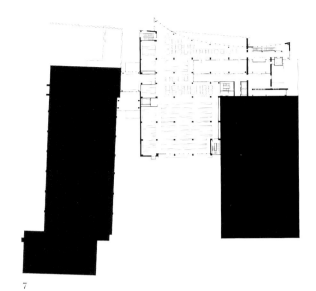

7

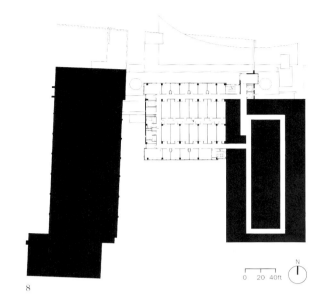

8

0   20   40ft   N

9

Lobbies at the eastern and western ends of the building are linked by an internal street which also provides additional natural light to the library. The 30-foot-high western lobby provides access from the north and south, and offers connections to all three buildings. On the research floors above, perimeter offices wrap a core of laboratory and support space for pharmacognosy, pharmaceutics, medicinal chemistry, biochemistry, molecular genetics and microbiology. Connections to existing floors provide continuity with the adjacent buildings.

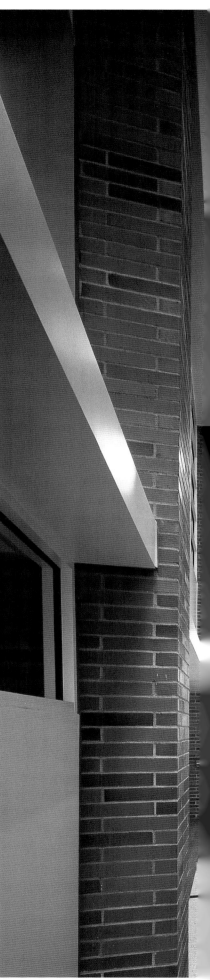

10

11

12

13

10 Interior perspective
11 East lobby
12 Spine
13 West lobby

Dongbu Central Research Institute

Design/Completion 1991/1995
Taejon, Korea
Dongbu Corporation
460,000 square feet
Concrete structure
Metal panel (manufactured by Dongbu)

Located at a major intersection in the Dae Duck Research Park in Taejon, 100 miles south of Seoul, the Central Research Institute is a new technical–administrative center for a large Korean manufacturer, Dongbu Corporation. The building houses research laboratories, administrative offices, and a pilot plant for product testing, expressed in intersecting forms set against the open vistas of the park. An artificial lake at the entry side creates dramatic reflections, doubling the building's scale and creating a bold image for the company. The building is proudly clad in the metal panel system manufactured by Dongbu.

A two-story pavilion used for administrative functions passes through the broad sweeping arc containing the research laboratories. At their intersection is a three-story lobby. Each formal element in the complex is able to expand independently in a linear fashion, without disrupting the existing functions— a requirement established by Dongbu in the master plan. The second phase of the extension would also include additional pilot plants, dormitories, and an auditorium and recreational facilities.

2

3

1

4

5

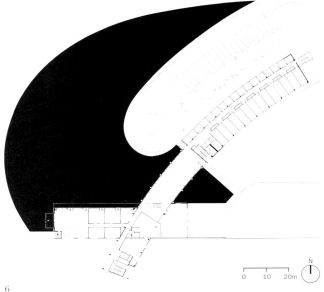

6

1   Exterior view from west
2   Interior view from second floor, looking west
3   Dusk view of building
4   Reception
5   Detail of entrance to laboratories
6   First floor plan
7   General view of the institute

7

Biomedical Research Building II, University of Pennsylvania

Design/Completion 1994/1999
Philadelphia, Pennsylvania
University of Pennsylvania
384,000 square feet
Steel structure
Glass, brick, and stone

The Biomedical Research Building houses many of the University of Pennsylvania's top medical research institutes in the fields of cancer, gene therapy, and reproductive biology. It completes the fourth corner of a research quadrangle and, with its expressed auditorium, creates a focus for the research center. The laboratories, office and support spaces occupy ten floors of the 14-story building, which for the purposes of efficiency and economy is rectangular in plan. It forms a backdrop for the more figural lobby and auditorium projecting into the quadrangle. Other public spaces include a medical bookstore and cafe, and the lobby is used for special functions as well as for lounge seating. The building materials reflect the traditional brick and limestone architecture of the campus, but are expressed in a way that is compatible with the scale of the building and technology of the research functions housed within.

1   View from east
2   Exterior corner detail

2

3

4

Biomedical Research Building II, University of Pennsylvania 95

6

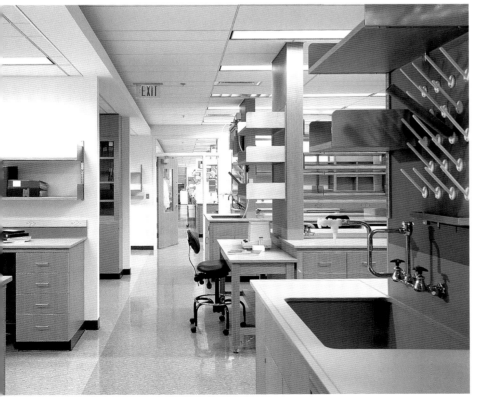

7

8

10

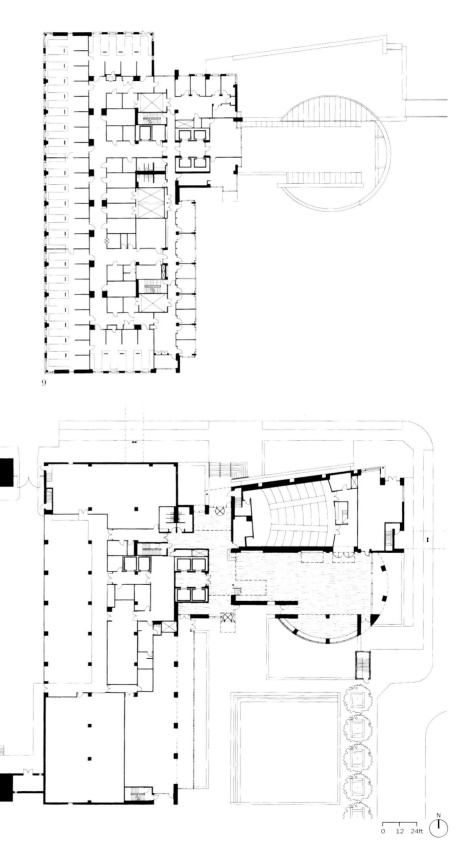

9

McDonnell Pediatric Research Building
Washington University in St.Louis

Design/Completion 1996/2000
St. Louis, Missouri
Washington University in St. Louis, School of Medicine
228,000 square feet
Reinforced concrete
Brick, limestone, painted aluminum curtain wall, and granite

The dense site and required spatial efficiencies of the labs in this building led to the design of a single block with a high degree of surface manipulation to achieve the same articulation of functions found in other similar projects. The building subtly adjusts to its site, and expresses its function through a series of wrapping layers of varying materials. The laboratory is located in the dense Washington Medical School campus, and is connected at its western face to a recently constructed animal facility. It contains laboratories, support space and offices for the pediatric biomedical and cancer research programs. Repetitive laboratory spaces are designed for maximum flexibility, suitable for a diverse range of users, and for adaptation to future research needs.

Continued

1   Aerial view of model
2   Model view of the main façade
3   Site plan

1

2

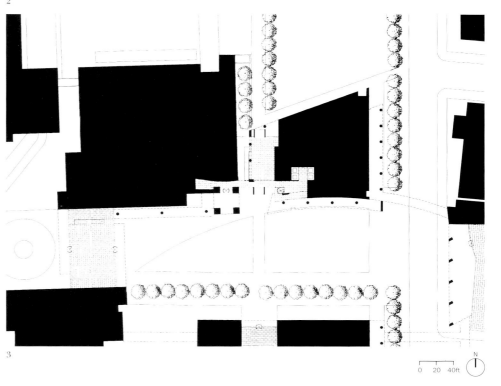

3

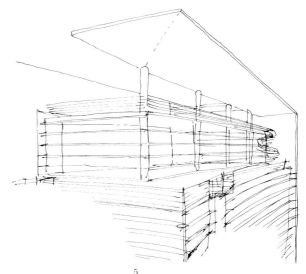

5

A gently curved, transparent curtain wall on the south façade allows offices and communal spaces to overlook the newly shaped quadrangle at the heart of the campus. It stops short of the adjacent building, in order to emphasize the entry lobby which connects through the building to the north. Strip windows in brick façades signify laboratory spaces on the north and east elevations. Stone, which is found in other buildings on campus, is used selectively at the entry, and to establish the southeast corner.

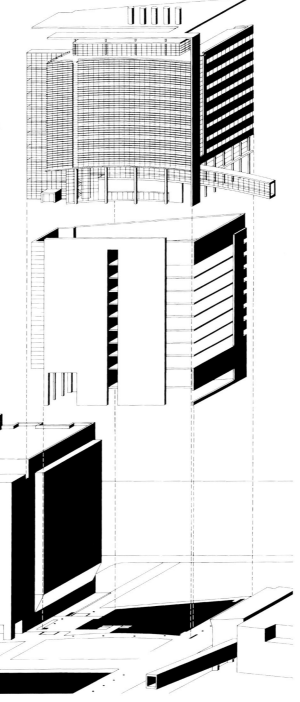

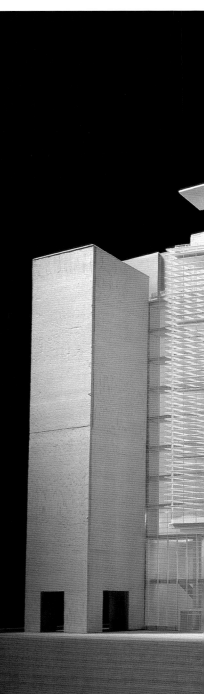

4

6

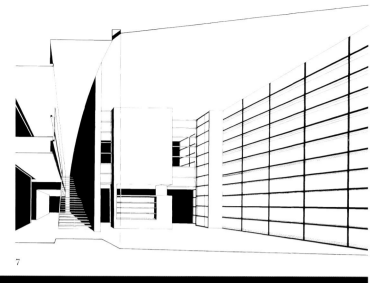

7

8

9

UCLA
Neurosciences Institute

Design/Completion 1997/2002
Los Angeles, California
University of California Los Angeles
130,000 square feet
Steel structure
Brick, precast concrete, and glass

This laboratory was initially identified in the Center for Health Sciences Redevelopment Study previously completed by Perkins & Will after the 1994 Northridge earthquake. The new facility supports the relocation of neuroscience programs of the Neuropsychiatric Institute and the School of Medicine, currently located in buildings damaged by the earthquake. The facility includes wet laboratories for neuroscientific and genetic research, support space, animal facilities, staff and research offices, and other instructional and public spaces.

The L-shaped site occupies a pivotal position on the academic campus, between the Medical Center Campus and the Court of Sciences, and provides the opportunity to connect these areas with exterior public space. There is a grade change of

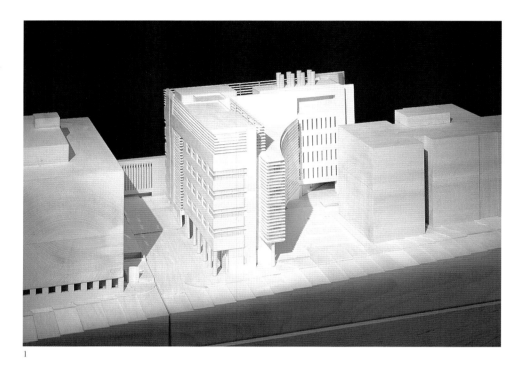

1

1   Model, view from south
2   View from east
3   Ground floor plan
4   View from southwest

2

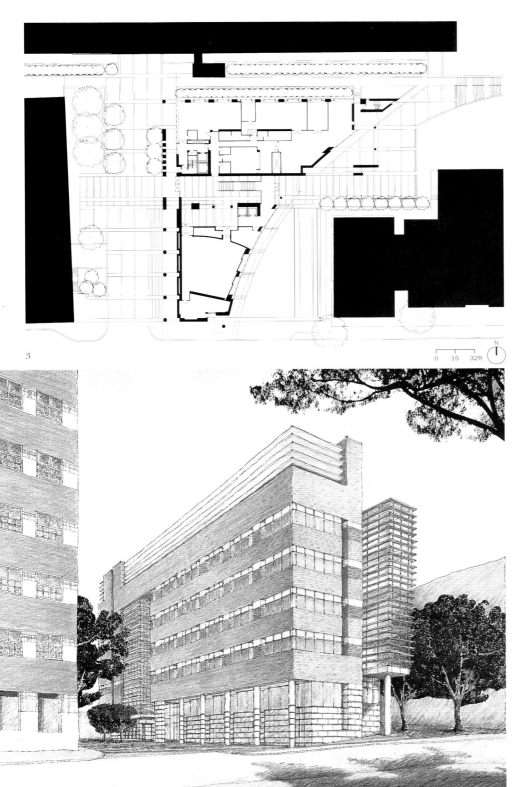

approximately 30 feet in the northeastern corner of the site, and the site continues to slope down another 11 feet to Young Drive, on its southern edge. The building's gentle curve pulls away from the adjacent buildings to create a continuous, cascading pedestrian space with entry to the Health Sciences building at its midpoint. This active public space also provides space between the buildings for adequate lighting and view. The centrally located, two-story lobby negotiates the grade change within the building by connecting east and west entrances with a cascading stair. The first-floor lobby provides access to the auditorium and offices, while the upper lobby serves second-floor interview and lab areas. Floors three through five are typical lab floors, with animal facilities on each floor.

3

0   16   32ft

N

4

Georgia Institute of Technology, Manufacturing Related Disciplines Complex, Phase II

Design/Completion 1998/2000
Atlanta, Georgia
Georgia Institute of Technology
130,000 square feet
Poured-in-place concrete frame with pan joist system
Brick, poured-in-place concrete, and aluminum panels

The Manufacturing Related Disciplines Complex Phase II (MRDC II) will be the new home for the School of Material Sciences Engineering, and it will provide additional facilities for the School of Mechanical Engineering at the Georgia Institute of Technology. The laboratory facility will be the largest of its kind in Atlanta, and one of the premier material sciences engineering research facilities in the country.

A sweeping curtain wall encloses a three-story glass lobby that links the two building wings like a sculptural lantern. Bridges spanning the space afford views down into the lobby, toward the Olympic aquatic center, and out into the student quadrangle. It provides an image for the building and the research complex.

The two wings house laboratories, student and faculty offices, and inter-disciplinary classrooms. The building's lab module was designed to provide maximum flexibility for multiple-lab arrangements, and maximum space efficiency. It will also accommodate the labs' future needs to change, grow, and move within the building. MRDC II has several special laboratories with unique features.
The high bay space in the Acoustics Department of the Mechanical Engineering Wing is a two-story volume housing a water tank and an echoic tank. The Impact Testing Lab accommodates a 53-foot-long gas gun. Three electron microscopes are located in the Microscopy Suite of the Material Sciences Department.

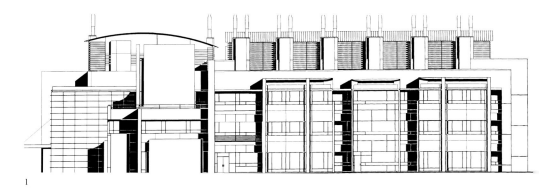

1

2

3

1 South elevation
2 Model view at main entrance
3 Site plan
4 West elevation
5 Rendering of main entrance
6 Perspective at west entry
7 Model view at courtyard

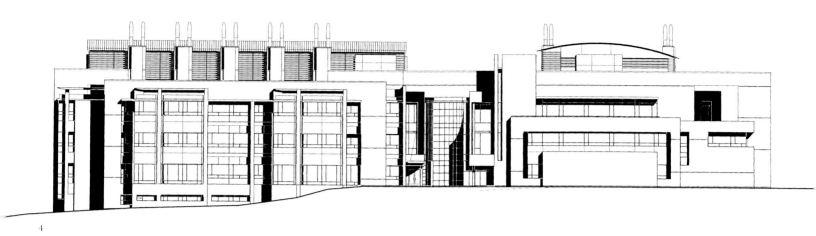

4

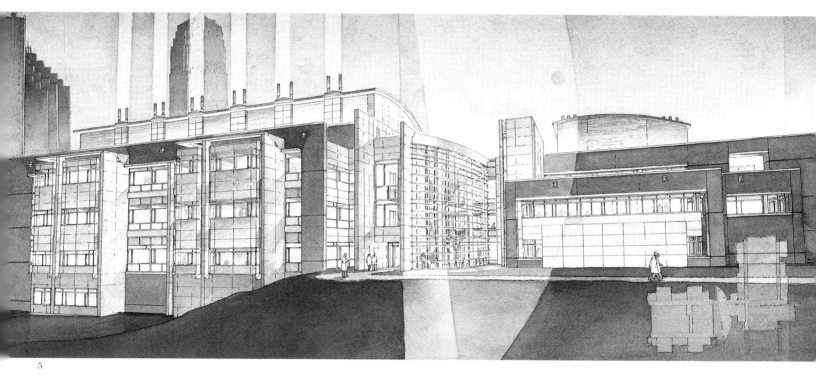

5

6

7

University of Southern California Neurogenetic Institute

Design/Completion: 1999/2001
Los Angeles, California
University of Southern California
125,000 square feet
Concrete structure
Architectural precast concrete, and aluminum and glass curtainwall

The Neurogenetic Institute is the first of three new buildings proposed in the master plan for the Research Quadrangle for the University of Southern California. Together, the three buildings will create a formal courtyard aligned with the entrance drive across San Pablo Street. The five research floors, basement animal facility and mechanical penthouse are organized in two interlocking 'L-shaped' bars which contain the laboratories and offices, respectively. The offices face south and east, with views toward the new courtyard and San Pablo Street. Laboratories line the northern and western façades, and are based on a modular planning concept which accommodates varying user requirements. Laboratory and building support occupy the interior of the block.

The entrance to the building is oriented to San Pablo Street. A six-story portal announces entry to the Institute from the south. The four-story, cantilevered bay window performs a similar function in the north. The exterior arcade addresses the scale of the pedestrian, shades interior functions, and allows the building to visually float above the entry plaza. Public functions, such as the lobby, coffee bar and conference center, occupy the first floor, along with specialized research labs.

The exterior wall has been designed to maximize natural lighting while screening the interior from direct sunlight. The treatment of the wall varies, depending on its solar orientation. Precast panels and windows alternate in a saw-tooth pattern on the southern elevation, to provide views from the offices while screening them from direct sunlight. On the northern elevation, horizontal strip windows introduce daylight to the laboratories, while vertical fins incorporated into the eastern and western curtain wall systems reduce the amount of direct sunlight into labs and offices in the morning and afternoon.

1

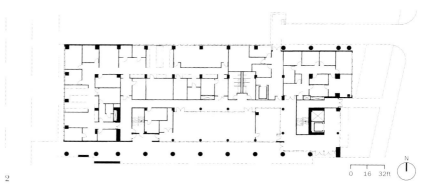

3

4

1   View from southeast
2   Ground floor plan
3   Model, aerial view from southeast
4   Typical laboratory

Thomas Jefferson University Cancer Center

Design/Completion 1999/2002
Philadelphia, Pennsylvania
Thomas Jefferson University
445,000 square feet
Steel structure
Brick, glass, stone, and metal roof

The Thomas Jefferson University Cancer Center for cancer treatment and research is located in central Philadelphia, on Locust Street between 10th and 11th streets. The form of the building resolves the conflict between expressing programmatic function, adjusting to a varied context and creating a cohesive whole. Its three major program elements are easily legible, through degrees of opacity/transparency. The private lab spaces are housed in an opaque masonry block along 11th Street; the more public clinic spaces along 10th Street are located in a glazed block lifted on columns; and the public lobby and lounge spaces, arranged as a series of two-story spaces, provide a bridge between the labs and clinic. Entrance to the main lobby is from the 10th Street end, under the raised clinic.

The building's plan and volumetric expression both respond to existing site conditions. The triangular shape of the plan adjusts to the disposition of adjacent campus structures, and defines a new central plaza for the campus. The sloping roof has a dual function: it responds in scale to the context, which ranges from five to 25 stories, and simultaneously unifies the three volumes it contains to create a single image for the Cancer Center.

1

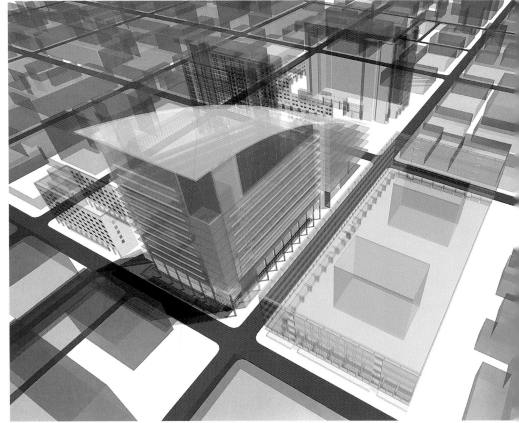

2

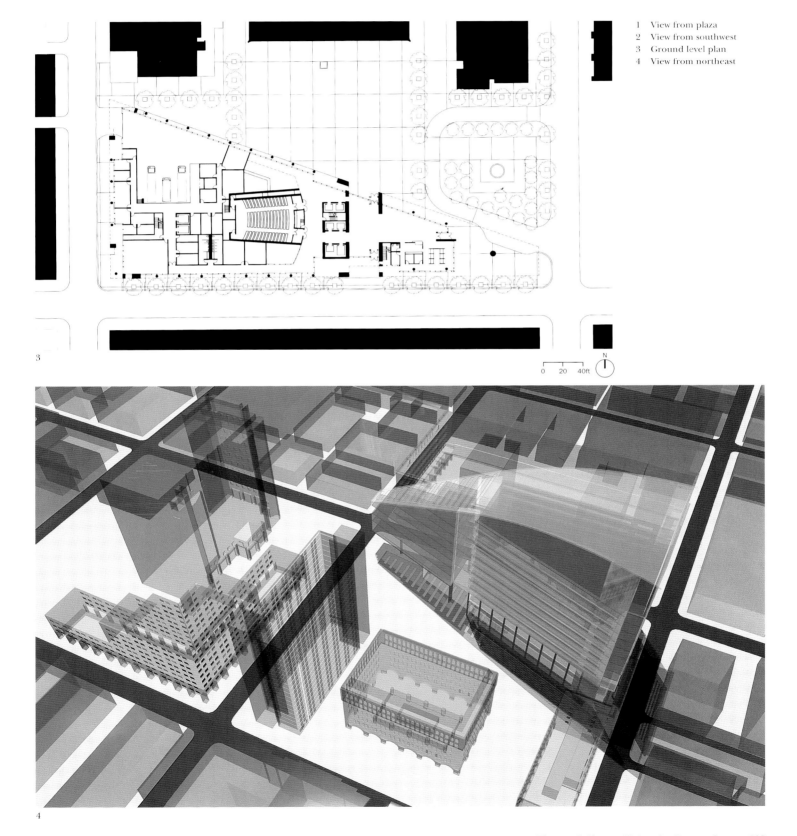

1 View from plaza
2 View from southwest
3 Ground level plan
4 View from northeast

0 20 40ft

N

3

4

Healthcare

Piedmont Hospital Rehabilitation and Fitness Center

Design/Completion 1988/1989
Atlanta, Georgia
Piedmont Hospital
33,000 square feet
Original structure is concrete, addition is steel with steel-truss roof structure
Brick, concrete block, glass and glass-block with painted metal frames

The Piedmont Hospital Rehabilitation and Fitness Center includes the renovation of an existing, 22,000-square-foot, 2-story structure, and an 11,000-square-foot addition. The program includes a recreational lap pool and a separate arthritis pool, a gymnasium, locker rooms, a circuit training area, and aerobics rooms.

This project is a new building type and an important revenue generator for Piedmont Hospital; therefore, capturing the attention of motorists on Peachtree Street was an important design goal. Expressing the building's structure with exposed trusses responds to this design goal, as well as to the functional goal of isolating the steel structure from chlorine gases in the pool. Hollow, precast planks suspended from the trusses form the roof over the pool area. A combination of glass and glass-block provides generous amounts of daylight to the pool areas, retail tenants, and office building, as well as high visibility at night. The brick and concrete-block colors relate to the existing building's limestone trim and insets.

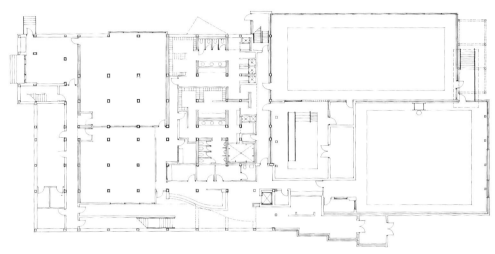

1

2

1   First floor plan
2   Pool exterior
3   Gym interior
Opposite:
    Corner exterior steel at pool   3

112

Hackensack Medical Center, Don Imus/WFAN Pediatric Center for Tomorrow's Children

Design/Completion 1989/1995
Hackensack, New Jersey
Hackensack Medical Center
90,000 square feet
Steel frame
Curtainwall, brick on masonry cavity wall, clerestory

The Don Imus/WFAN Pediatric Center is one of three new buildings identified on Perkins & Will's master facilities plan for Hackensack Medical Center. The Center is the largest facility providing sophisticated, outpatient cancer care for children in the eastern United States. Examination and treatment areas provide a new home for the children's cancer clinic, and programs for pediatric behavioral medicine. The 4-story facility is designed to create a colorful, humane environment for children and their parents.

The building is divided into two distinct wings. Office and meeting spaces are contained in the wing to the north of the atrium, while clinical spaces are housed in the wing closest to the hospital. The atrium marks a new entry sequence to the large medical center campus, and orients the patient and visitors, since it is viewed from waiting areas on all levels. The tree-like columns are playful elements in the space. The building's location at the crest of a hill on the campus edge affords dramatic views, and light enters all spaces in the facility to help provide a healing atmosphere.

1

2

0   10   20ft

N

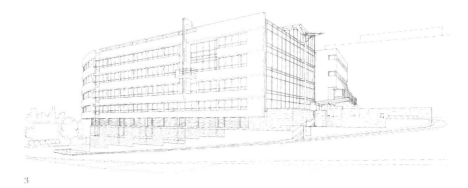

3

4

1   View of entry from west
2   Entry level floor plan
3   Perspective
4   View from northwest

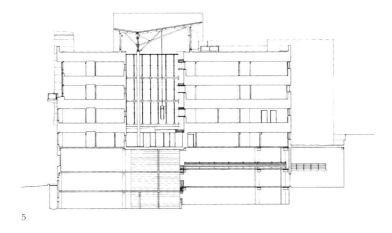

5

6

7

8

Sharon Hospital

Design/ Completion 1992/1995
Sharon, Connecticut
Sharon Hospital
60,000 square feet addition/ 30,000 square feet renovation
Steel frame
Curtainwall, brick on masonry cavity wall, aluminum panel

Sharon Hospital is a 92-bed facility located in rural Connecticut. The project included renovations to an existing building and an addition to accommodate outpatient functions, surgery, and a 32-bed nursing unit. Originally inpatient-oriented, the physical plant was transformed into an outpatient-focused facility. Clear public circulation and separation of outpatients from inpatients and staff were important functional goals.

The design of the addition is conceived of as a series of parallel building blocks bracketed by an interior circulation spine and an exterior public corridor. Originating from the new lobby and entry at one end, the interior spine extends into the landscape at the other end, allowing for future growth. Outpatient departments are entered from the exterior corridor, creating a dual circulation system. This design solution results in a series of articulated blocks, related in scale and arrangement to the large, private residences of the area. Architectural features of these residences, such as the enclosed porch, grand reception hall and carriageway, are reinterpreted in a

Continued

1

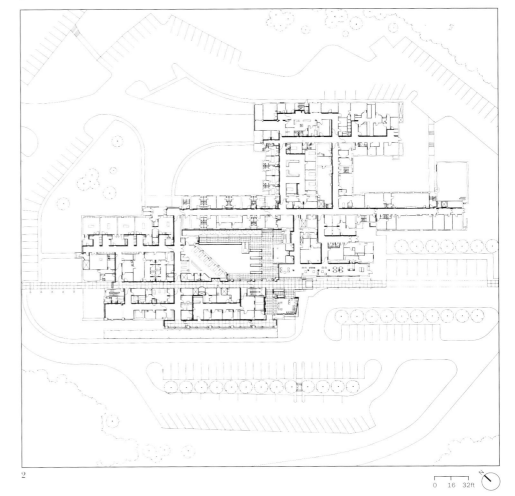

2

1   View from the south
2   First floor plan
Opposite:
    View of sunshades and glazing

0   16   32ft

modernist vocabulary in the outpatient corridor, 2-story lobby, and entry canopy. These special elements connect the new and existing buildings, orient the visitor, and provide an exciting public sequence. The exterior skin of masonry, glazing, aluminum panels and sunshades wraps and unifies the new entry wing. Its vocabulary extends into the building in the detailing of reception and nursing desks.

4

5

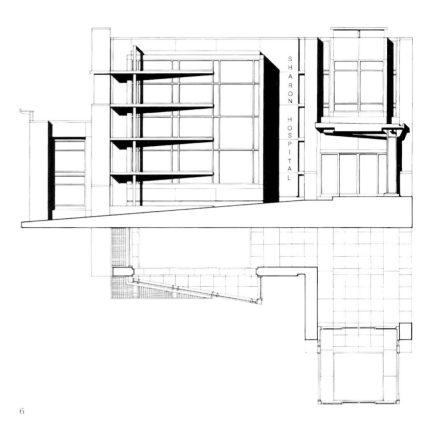

6

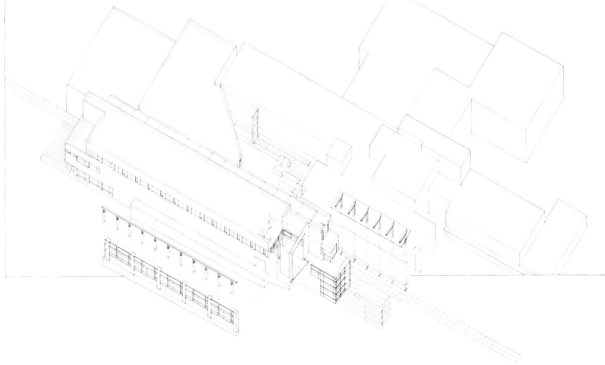

7

8 Interior perspective of lobby
9 Details of the reception desk
Opposite:
 Two-story lobby with views to the surrounding
 landscape

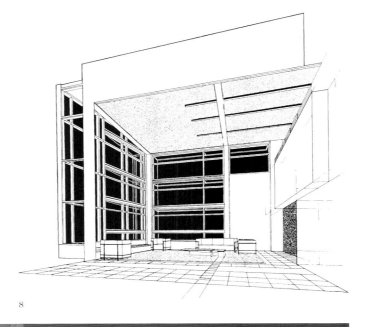

8

9

South Georgia Medical Center, Pearlman Cancer Center

Design/Completion 1995/1996
Valdosta, Georgia
South Georgia Medical Center
28,000 square feet
Concrete slab-on-grade, steel frame, composite slab roof
Stucco, aluminum storefront and aluminum curtainwall,
composite building panels

The Pearlman Cancer Center includes both new construction and renovated space. The Center is attached to the hospital building on the northeast end of the campus, and provides a dedicated entrance, entry drive, and parking for cancer patients. The addition augments existing radiation oncology services by providing space for medical oncology services including infusion therapy, a satellite lab, shared examination space, dietary and social services consulting, patient education, and activity areas. Also included are a large conference room, physician billing, and a physician office suite. The addition creates two open courtyards accessible to patients and staff.

1

2

1 East elevation
2 Interior view of entry
3 Axonometric
4 Night-time view of gallery and entry

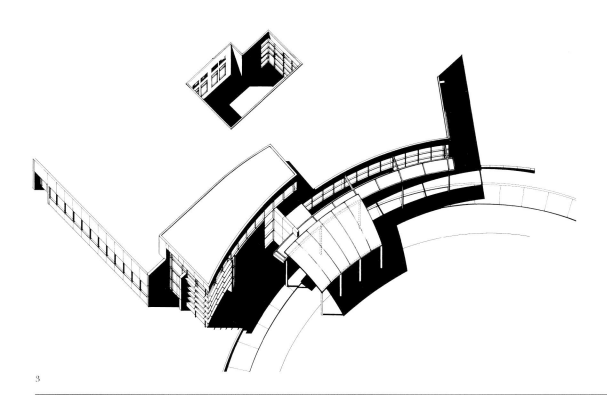

3

4

Florida Hospital, Heartland Medical Center

Design/Completion 1995/1997, renovation 1999
Sebring, Florida
Florida Hospital
235,000 square feet
Structural steel
Polymer modified exterior finish system (synthetic stucco),
aluminum curtainwall system

The new Florida Hospital Heartland
Medical Center is a freestanding
replacement facility on an 85-acre site that
is fully developed, with water features and
landscaping interspersed with paths. This
outdoor contemplative and wellness space
also provides views for patients and staff.
The facility has 101 acute-care inpatient
beds, with extensive outpatient services
to accommodate the steady growth of the
south central Florida (Heartland) region.
The building design allows for vertical and
horizontal expansion to accommodate this
growth.

Continued

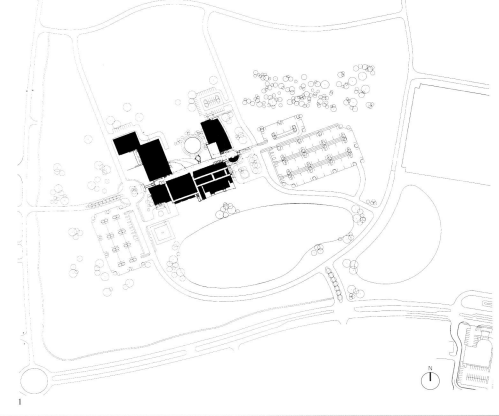

1

2

3

4

5

1   Site plan
2   View across lake at daytime
3   South elevation with palm trees
4   View of courtyard
5   Detail at terraces

The medical center and medical office building have 200,000 and 30,000 square feet of space, respectively. All office and clinical spaces are interconnected in order to provide easy access. The facility also includes an intensive care/cardiac unit, birthing suites, pediatric unit, surgical suites, fitness center and trail, and community education center and library. The Wellness Center/Health Education Center/Exercise and Fitness Center are at the "front door" of the complex, to encourage awareness and interaction with everyone arriving at the center.

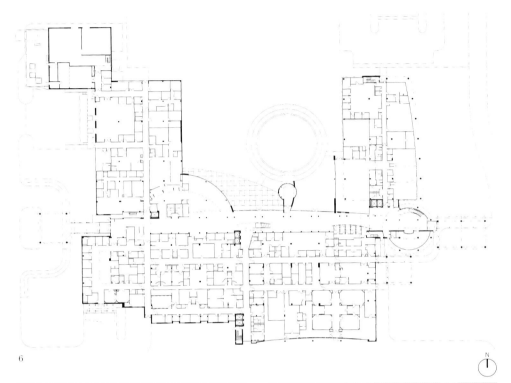

6

N

7

8

9

10

6   First floor plan
7   Courtyard pool view at night
8   Inpatient entry canopy
9   Interior gallery
10 View across lake at dawn
11 East elevation

11

MidState Medical Center

Design/ Completion 1995/1998
Meriden, Connecticut
MidState Medical Center
237,000 square feet
Steel frame, exposed steel structure at exterior canopies
Aluminum curtainwall with painted finish, Norman brick on masonry cavity wall, painted aluminum panel

The MidState Medical Center is the first new stand-alone hospital to be built in New England in two decades. The goal of this project was to streamline the operations of two aging facilities, with primary focus on efficiency, future flexibility, physician integration, and patient-focused service. It was important that the building maintain a sense of civic importance while creating an intimate, patient-friendly environment that is sensitive to its New England context.

The site is located at the junction of a major interstate and a main traffic artery, offering a strong presence in the community. The siting strategy draws from traditional New England town planning, by laying a grid over the natural topography of the site. This grid ties the building circulation—seen as a series of interior streets—to the organization of the parking and landscaping. A "main street," or galleria, acts as the main public circulation spine, and a "town green" creates a ceremonial and functional entry forecourt.

Continued

1

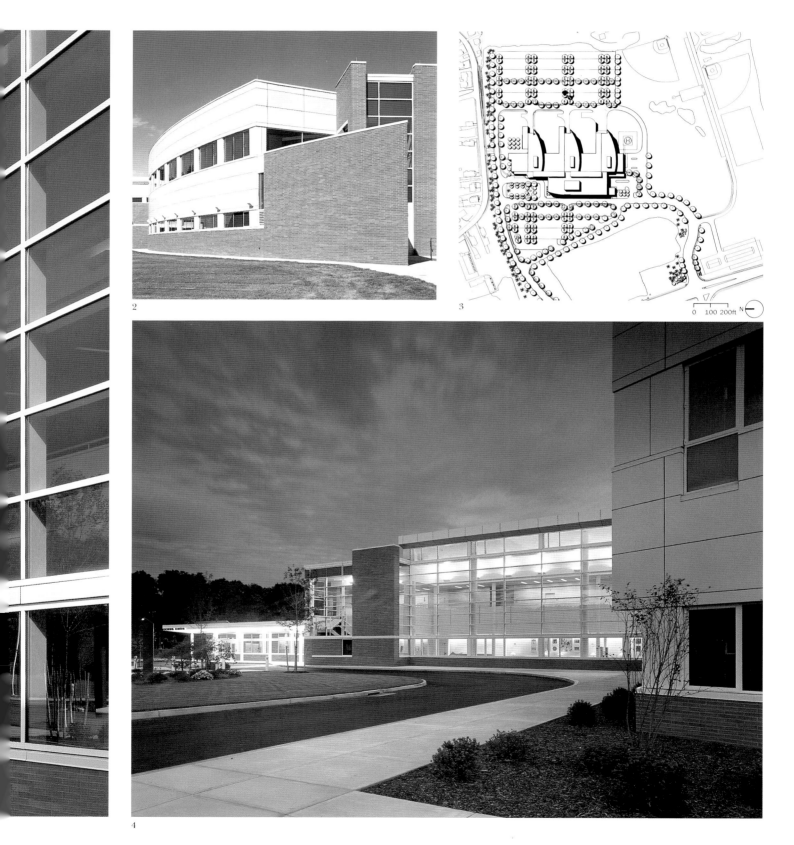

2

3

0   100 200ft   N

4

5

6

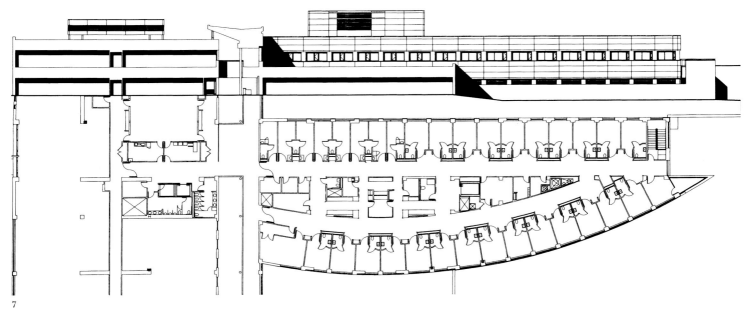

7

The building is composed of three distinct components: the diagnostic and treatment block, the medical office building, and the patient-care pavilions. These components are organized along two spines, the major public galleria for outpatient and visitor circulation, and an inpatient spine for staff and inpatient travel. The spines are open at either end, to provide views into the landscape while allowing for the hospital functions to expand freely as needed for future growth. The three patient-care pavilions are located above the diagnostic and treatment block, with access from the galleria along an open balcony. Bridges from the medical office building to the patient-care pavilions occur at the entry points to each pavilion.

The exterior articulation and materials reinforce the building's organization and emphasize the building as an assemblage of distinct parts. The rectilinear surfaces are faced in a brick which relates to the reddish–orange outcroppings out of the nearby foothills, while light-colored metal panels cladding the curved planes of the building, and curtainwall elements provide a sense of lightness and openness to the circulation and patient areas.

8

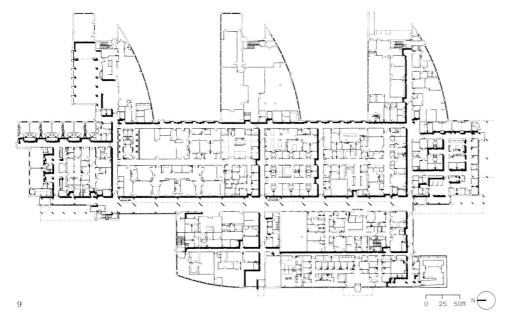

9

0   25   50ft   N

University of Illinois at Chicago, Ambulatory Care Facility

Design/Completion 1995/1999
Chicago, Illinois
University of Illinois at Chicago
240,000 square feet
Steel structure
Brick, aluminum and glass curtainwall

The new Ambulatory Care Facility forms an aesthetic and physical link between several buildings on the University of Illinois at Chicago's dense medical campus, southwest of downtown Chicago. By connecting various separated facilities, it creates a functionally cohesive system, as well as a single visual image for the Medical Center.

The site is west of the existing hospital, and spans Taylor Street in the north–south direction. This location allows the large floor plates required for operational efficiency, and also provides the opportunity to link adjacent buildings. The main entrance lobby is on the south side of Taylor Street, and connects to the main public corridor which runs along the east side of the building across Taylor Street, above the first floor. Not only does this separate public corridor minimize traffic through the clinics, but it also provides orientation, views, and light. Its continuous band of curtainwall suggests the functional cohesiveness of the complex, and conveys the desired image of a modern treatment facility.

Internally, the facility is organized around a center concept with functionally related clinics grouped to share clinical and administrative support spaces. The centers are designed as modular units, with universal examination, procedure, and consultation rooms.

1

2

1   View from southeast
2   Aerial view looking west
Opposite:
    Street level view of bridge connections

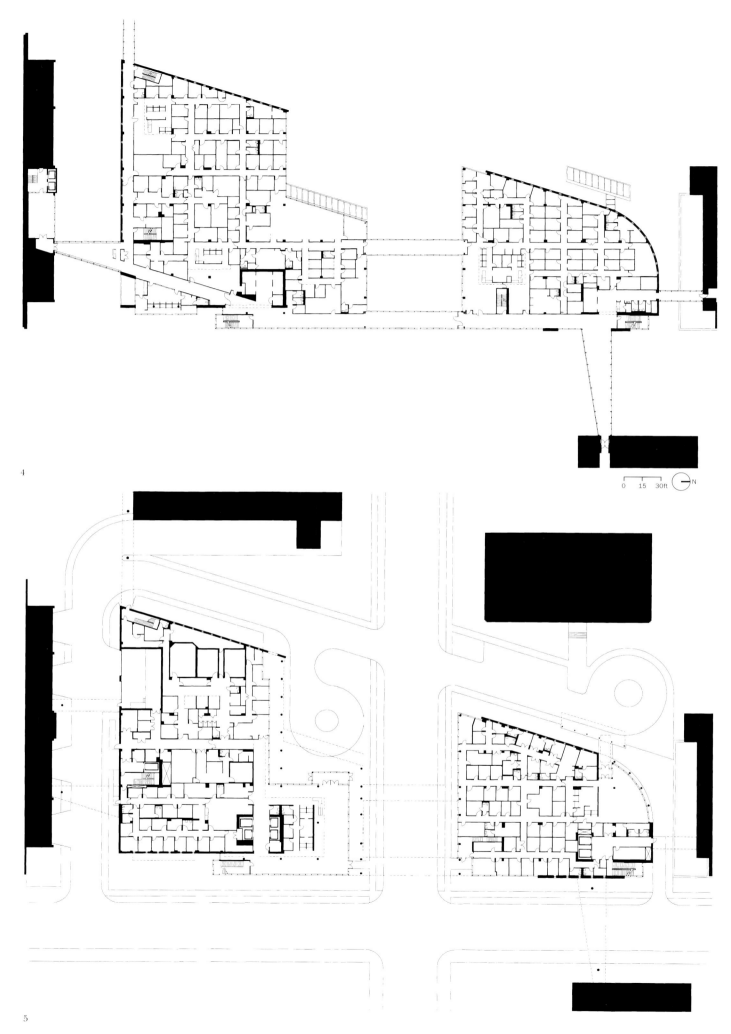

4

0   15   30ft   N

5

6

8

7

9

4 Second floor plan
5 First floor plan, site plan
6 Bridge view of connections over Taylor Street
7 Aerial view looking east
8 Stair
9 Main lobby

UCLA, Health Sciences Campus
120-day Master Plan Study

Design/Completion 1996
Los Angeles, California
University of California Los Angeles
Approximately 2.9m square feet of new space

An architectural and engineering review of UCLA's Center for Health Sciences (CHS), conducted after the 1994 Northridge earthquake, recommended the replacement of major portions of the complex as the most cost-effective method for ensuring continued operation of the facilities in the event of a future large earthquake. Perkins & Will was commissioned to provide master planning studies that included the development of a physical master site plan, planning and massing studies, and a phasing plan for a new academic medical complex at the University. The master plan project was completed within 120 days, as mandated by the University's accelerated schedule.

The goal of the master plan was to develop a concept that would unite the new hospital, research, and medical education components within a comprehensive master plan that could be implemented quickly and with minimum impact to continuing operations. In addition, an important goal was to create significant outdoor spaces of varying scales that would extend the core academic campus environment to the south. The final design creates an arc of buildings, which represents the relationship of all the components of the health campus and defines new exterior spaces, including a new "public square" for the medical campus.

During the master planning process, 11 sites were studied for the replacement hospital. The site chosen was on Westwood Boulevard, adjacent to the existing ambulatory care center. The new building will become a gateway to the campus. Perkins & Will, in association with Pei, Cobb, Freed & Partners and RBB, is currently working on the design and construction of the Westwood Replacement Hospital.

1

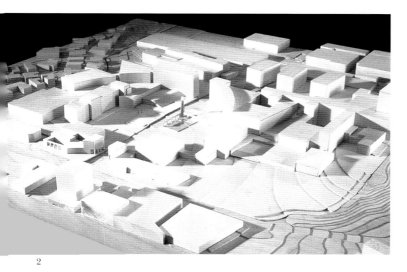

2

3

4

1   Overall view
2   View looking north
3   Aerial view of model
4   Proposed site plan

The CORE Center AIDS/HIV Clinic

Design/Completion 1996/1998
Chicago, Illinois
Cook County Bureau of Health Services
& Rush-Presbyterian–St. Luke's Medical Center
60,000 square feet
Steel structure
Brick, aluminum and glass curtainwall

This project is the United States' first freestanding, specialized outpatient clinic for persons with HIV/AIDS, tuberculosis, and other related infectious diseases. The building combines the resources of the largest public and private hospitals in the State, to provide comprehensive prevention, research, and treatment services and, in doing so, it is a model for the future of infectious disease care. The Center also serves as the referral and resource hub for a growing network of public and private community-based healthcare providers.

The building's design embodies the philosophy that treatment of communicable diseases such as AIDS should involve family and community in the healing process. Through brick color and details, the building suggests neighborhood scale, warmth, and familiarity. A gently curving wall around the first floor brings the building to the scale of the pedestrian, and encloses the screening clinic for at-risk patients. At the same time, the up-turned roofs provide a clear symbol of hope and optimism, easily read at the scale of the highway which passes the building to the north.

Continued

1

1 View of entry
2 Sketch
3 Entry view at dusk
4 View from west

2

3

4

5   Infusion therapy center
6   Typical floor plan
7   First floor plan
Opposite:
    Lobby and donor wall

The 4-story building is organized vertically around a central light-filled space, in order to minimize travel distances and to create a clear focal point for the varied functions. This gathering space is used to display the work of community artists. Patients are separated vertically by acuity levels. The screening clinic and public services such as a pharmacy and library occupy the first floor, while the fourth floor is the most private, designed for very ill patients. A conscious effort was made to provide light and space for the infusion room at the top of the building, where the most critical patients are treated.

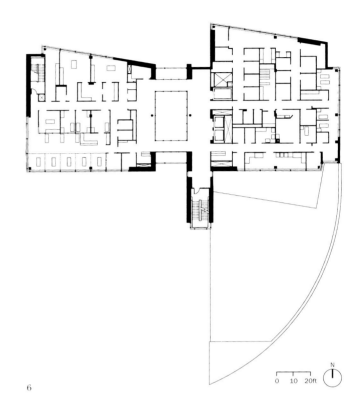

6

0   10   20ft

5

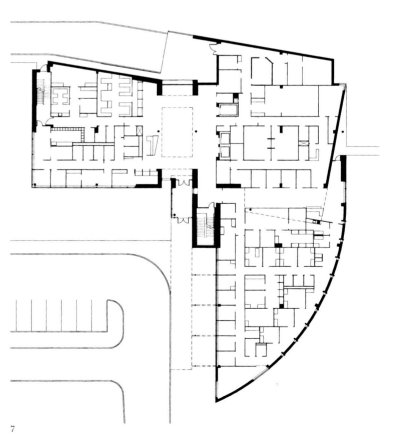

7

142

Corporate Office

Morton International Building
(100 N. Riverside Plaza)

Design/Completion 1987/1990
Chicago, Illinois
Orix Real Estate Equities
1,031,108 square feet
Steel frame with concrete platform
Curtainwall: gray granite, metal spandrel

The design for this 36-story high-rise allows the unusual site conditions and varied program requirements to be expressed through separate components that not only solve functional problems but also create symbolic elements that describe the building's relationship to the city. The site is an air-rights site over an operating railroad yard, situated along the west side of the Chicago River, and across from the downtown "Loop". Due to existing track configurations, foundations could be located only sporadically. The program consists of a leasable, 23-story tower, a 6-story data center for Illinois Bell Telephone with higher floor-to-floor height requirements, a parking garage for 435 cars, and a street-level restaurant.

The building's massing is a series of vertically stacked, rectilinear blocks, each housing an individual function. Layered onto the basic massing are a glazed loggia and a vertical clock tower that emphasize orientation toward the river and represent, in abstract form, the kinds of traditional architectural features found on many buildings along the river. An exterior public arcade and riverside promenade

Continued

1

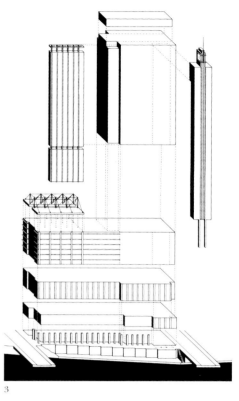

3

4

1 View from the Chicago River
2 Terrace at penthouse level
3 Exploded axonometric
4 View from the north

extend existing pedestrian circulation at the street level, and lead to access to a public park across the river. The curtainwall is a richly textured layering of horizontal and vertical bands of granite and metal spandrel, and structural elements, designed to simultaneously express the functions within and to weave them into a whole that suggests overlapping massing. The lower portion of the building, housing the telephone company data center, is actually cantilevered at the southwest corner from the exposed trusses above. From the south, these trusses recall the structure of the bridges across the river.

The lobby continues the theme of complex overlapping spaces, necessitated in part by the site limitations. The elevator lobby was raised to mezzanine level in order to allow the elevator pits to clear the railroad tracks below the building, leading to a 2-story lobby linked by a sculptural stair.

5

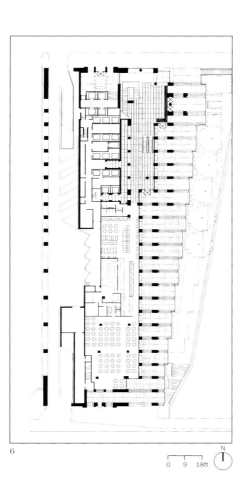

6

0   9   18ft

N

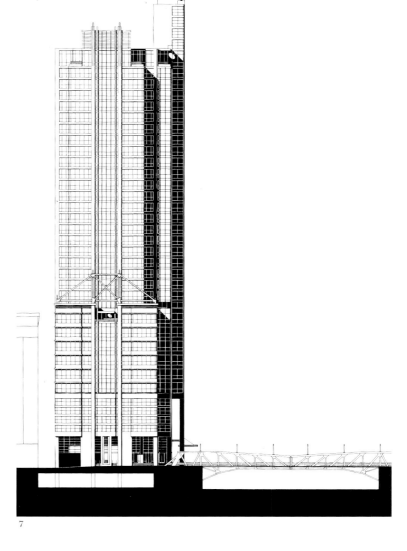

7

8

9

Sears Integrated Business Headquarters and Expansion

Design/Completion 1989/1992
Hoffman Estates, Illinois
Sears Integrated Business
1,977,000 square feet
Steel frame with composite concrete and metal deck
Reflective glass curtainwall

When the Sears Integrated Business group elected to leave its offices in the world's tallest building, in favor of a suburban campus, the company sought a significant change in image and internal function, as well as a physical relocation. The design of the new headquarters separates the large office program into several wings, in order to foster a comfortable, small-town culture appropriate to the company's new image.

In plan organization, the building is a modified pinwheel, with the 5- and 7-story building wings joined by a central atrium, or Main Street. People pass through this skylit space as they move from office space to conference space, training space, testing laboratories, and cafeteria and fitness center. This encourages employee communication. Reflective glass on the exterior curtainwall dematerializes the building and reflects the landscape and changing light, further breaking down the scale of the building.

1

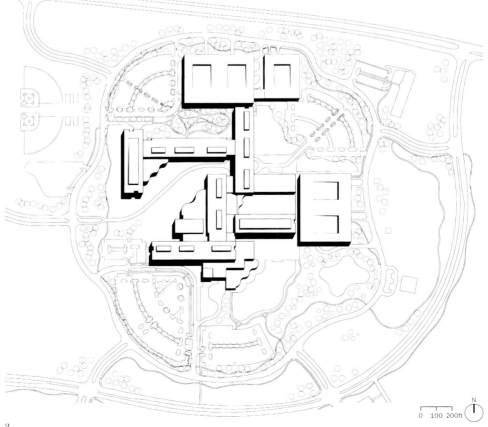

2

0 100 200ft
N

3

4

5

6

1 View towards entry from east
2 Site plan
3 West elevation
4 Five-story atrium at entrance
5 Water feature in atrium
6 Atrium, looking south

AMA Tower

Design/Completion 1995/2001
Manila, Philippines
AMA Land–Daewoo Corporation, Engineering & Construction
441,000 square feet including parking
Concrete structure
Steel, glass, granite

Located in one of the fastest-growing areas in Manila, adjacent to a major expressway interchange, this 37-story office tower seeks to create a distinct visual identity at a large scale. The curved north façade accentuates an overall image of streamlined verticality, and gives the impression of a shield suspended against the expressway. A composition of interlocking forms subtly differentiates the various programmatic elements and gives the building a directionality that anchors it specifically to the site. The curved prow is highlighted by its expressed tectonic components: exposed steel frame, wind-bracing and tie-rods. The double-height lobby and commercial space, mid-section of office floors, and penthouse and mechanical floors are clearly expressed in the façades. Six levels below grade are parking and mechanical spaces, and a helipad hovers above the roof level.

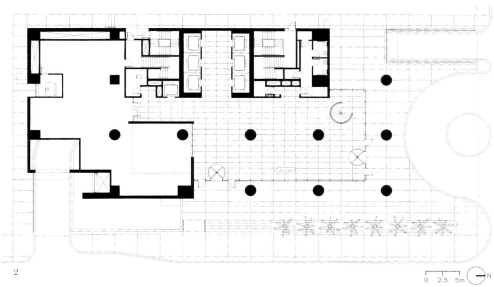

1

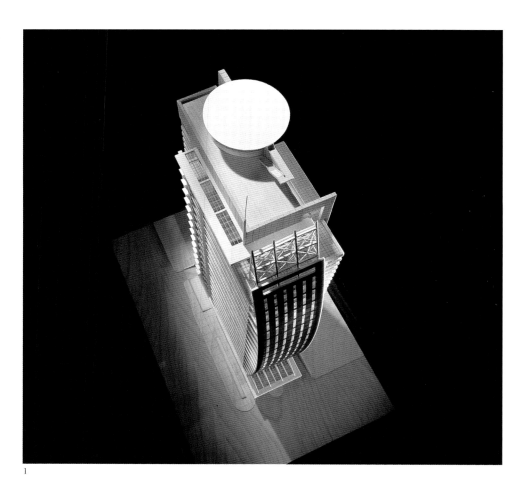

2

0   2.5   5m   N

3

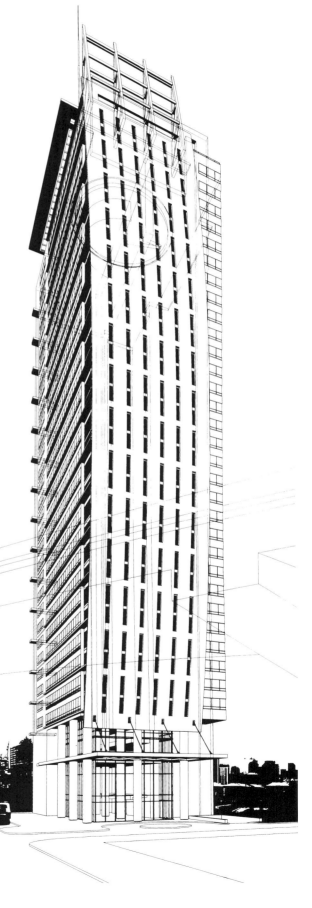

4

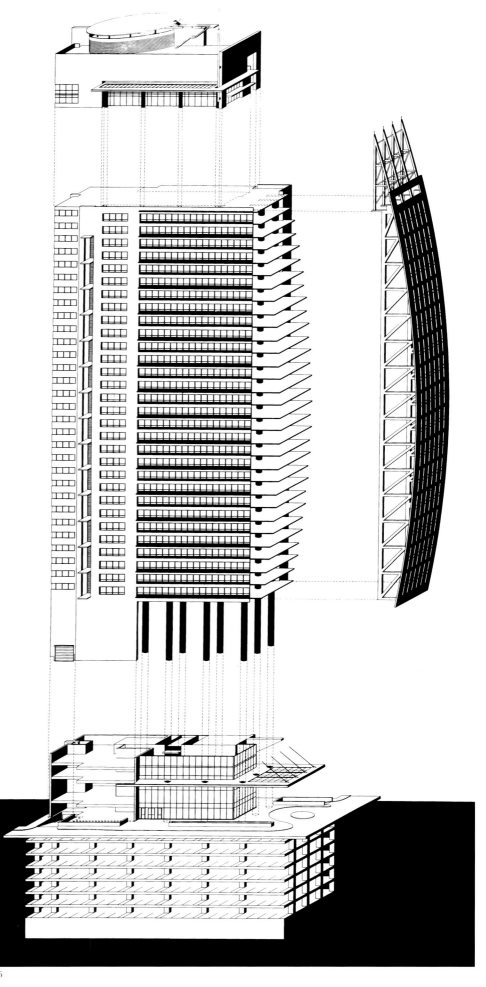

5   Photomontage of tower in Mandalyong area
6   Exploded axonometric
7   East elevation
8   Sketch

5

6

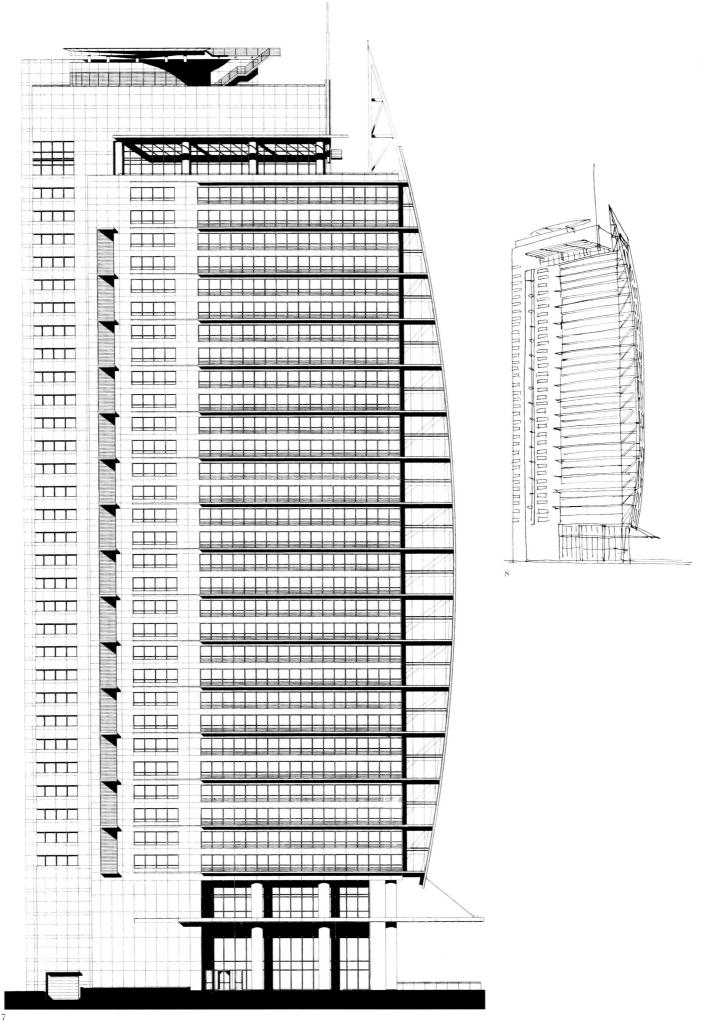

7

8

Grainger, Inc. Headquarters

Design/Completion 1996/1999
Lake Forest, Illinois
Grainger, Inc.
800,000 square feet
Fabricated structural steel
Glazed aluminum curtainwall, Pilkington glass curtainwall,
granite and limestone

Sited on a rise of land running parallel to dense woodland to the southwest, this new headquarters for Grainger, Inc. overlooks open field and wetlands to the northeast. The plan organization in which the two office wings are splayed apart by an atrium, responds to this natural siting, satisfies the requirement for large flexible office floor plates, and sets up a strategy for expansion in two additional phases. Successive phases will continue the gentle fanning of office buildings along the woodland edge.

The building suggests a strong relationship with its site, through long horizontal massing and the natural palette of granite and limestone cladding. Projecting granite fin walls at the ends of the office wings appear to literally anchor the building to the earth, and the undercut base and set-back top story, with cantilevered roof, emphasize horizontality and bring scale to the building. At the same time, the building responds to the high-tech and large-scale image of its client, an international distributor of electrical and machine parts.

1

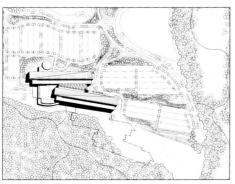

2

3

0   200   400ft

N

1 North façade, looking west
2 Site plan
3 View of entry at dusk
4 View towards complex from north
5 Detail at east wing

4

5

6

The taut exterior skin, sunscreens, exposed structure, expressed circulation, and extensive use of glass in the atrium suggest a machine aesthetic, and clear-span structure in the office wings allows for total flexibility in office planning.

Entry is along the edge of the atrium, which is treated almost as an exterior sunlit space between two stone-clad buildings. The atrium connects to the low-curved dining pavilion at its western end. There is a separate drop-off and entry access to the circular auditorium.

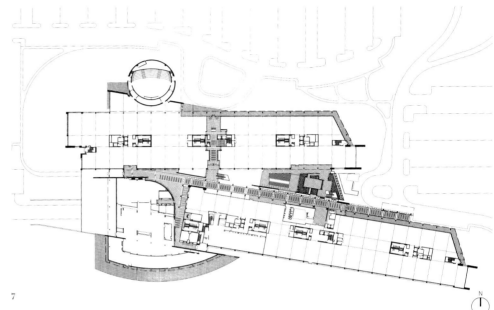

7

N

8

9

10

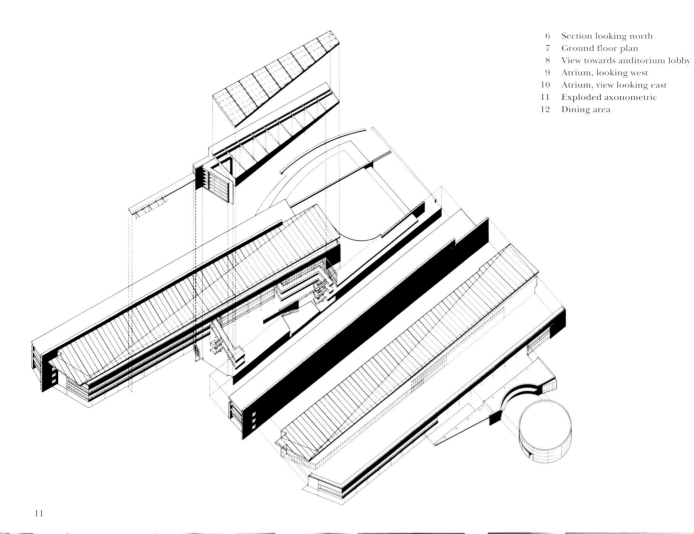

11

12

13

14

15

17

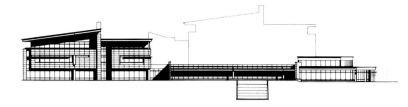

16

Burroughs Wellcome Fund

Design/Completion 1996/1999
Research Triangle Park, North Carolina
Burroughs Wellcome Fund
34,000 square feet
Steel frame
Limestone, sandstone

The Burroughs Wellcome Fund oversees the disbursement of grants to individuals engaged in medical research. The new facility is designed to provide office space for a staff of 30, as well as a place for convening the Fund's board, and conducting conferences within the scientific community.

The major formal spaces, including library and living room, are organized around an arcaded interior courtyard, landscaped with native plants. The remaining offices are organized in a series of stepped forms, which face the landscape preserve to the north, south, and west. At the east end of the building are the multi-purpose room, the boardroom, and the teleconference room. The building has a geometric discipline that orders all the spaces, both in plan and in elevation. This may be recognized most easily in the arcade surrounding the garden. Stone detailing emphasizes the underlying ordering system.

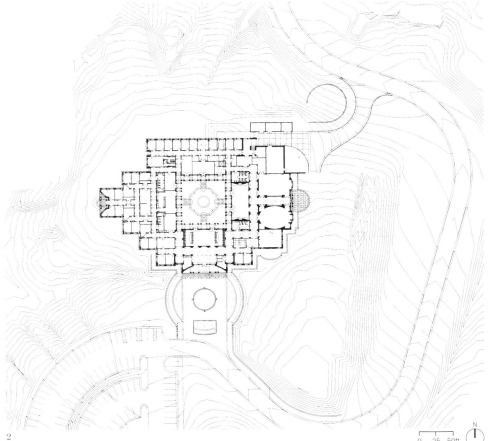

1

1   Courtyard at dusk
2   Site plan

2

N
0   25   50ft

North Carolina Biotechnology Center

Design/Completion 1988/1992
Research Triangle Park, North Carolina
North Carolina Biotechnology Center
47,000 square feet
Steel frame, lightweight concrete-floor slab on composite steel decking
Wood-molded brick, northern pink Minnesota limestone, green tint glass,
glass block

This conference and education center provides the setting for statewide support of biotechnology research and development. The building houses the Program Management Center's administrative offices, and a Conference and Education Center which serves outreach and education programs for the biotechnology community. The Center includes an auditorium, teleconference center and boardroom.

The site is a heavily wooded knoll, with steeply sloping sides to the north, east and west. The building's triangular plan complements the shape of the site and is accessed by an entry drive from the south. Offices overlook a preserve along the building's diagonal face and are separated from the Conference Center by a continuous, two-story galleria. The auditorium is expressed as a cylinder intersecting the building's east face. This organization satisfies the client's need for a clear visual and functional distinction between the two programmatic elements. Natural light and ventilation, energy conservation and access to the outdoors were also important considerations. The offices and Conference Center each have their own exterior space. To the east of the Conference Center, the trellises that rim the inside of the curved garden wall are draped in yellow jasmine and are shaded by trees, providing an outdoor setting for conference functions.

1

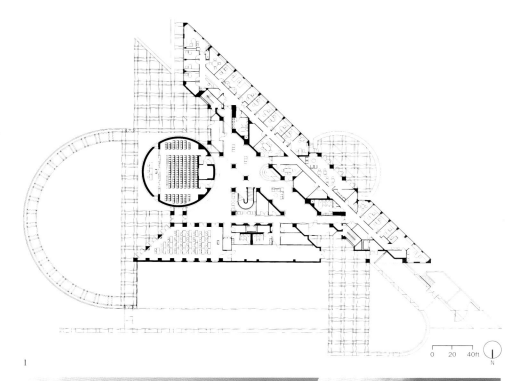

2

1   Lower level floor plan
2   View from north

Motorola Office and Manufacturing Building

Design/Completion 1997
Suburban Chicago, Illinois
Motorola
535,000 square feet
Fabricated structural steel
Corrugated metal panel and foam-backed metal panel, glazed aluminum
curtainwall

This facility, which houses light-assembly manufacturing, general office, and laboratory space, was designed to consolidate several satellite offices onto a 130-acre site northwest of Chicago. It is sited to preserve a stand of about 50 mature oak trees.

Three floors of office/laboratory spaces wrap the east and south sides of the manufacturing floor, and are separated from the manufacturing space by an internal skylit corridor, or pedestrian "street". This highly transparent space visually connects the factory and office, and reinforces the idea that the facility functions as a whole rather than as a collection of discrete elements. On the ground floor this spine connects all public areas, such as the conference center, cafeteria, store, customer salon, and training areas. Walkways, bridges, and cascading stairs connect to the upper floors and activate the space. The building, with its taut, linear skin and horizontal expression, appears to float on the prairie landscape. At the visitor entrance, the glazed conference center, with its overhanging roof, projects out over the pond. The cafeteria visually terminates the far end of the building.

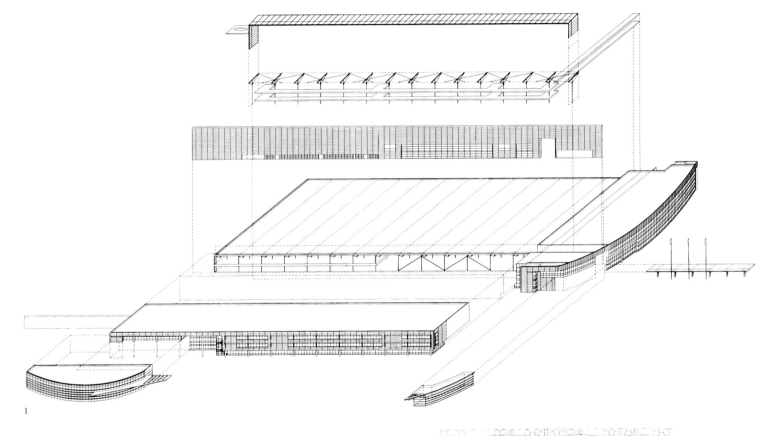

1

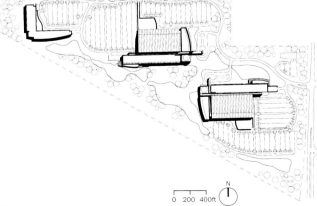

1   Exploded axonometric
2   Site plan
3   View, looking northwest
4   Bird's-eye view at night
5   View of entry from east

2

3

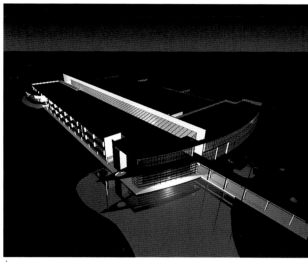

4

5

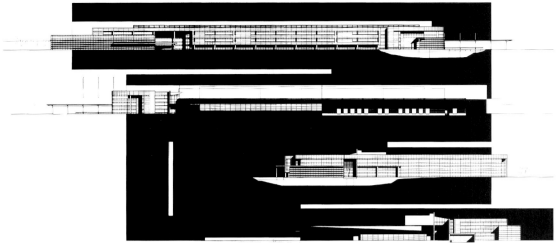

6

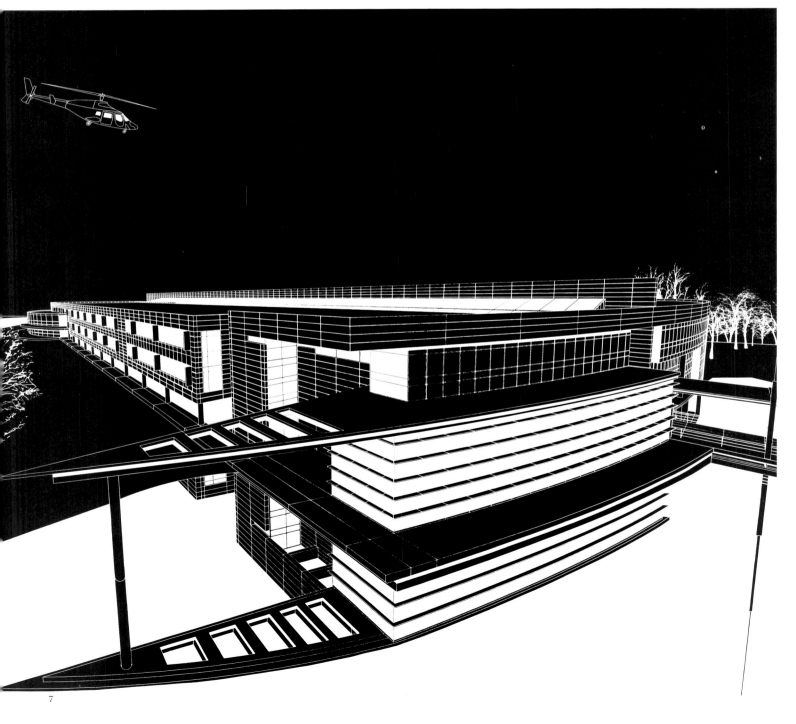

7

8

9

MetroBank Headquarters

Design/Completion 1997
Manila, Philippines
Metropolitan Bank
625,000 square feet
Concrete structure
Glass, metal panels, granite

Urban design considerations and ecological sensitivity are the two factors most influential on the form of the MetroBank Headquarters designed for Manila. The headquarters was to be a mixed-use development including office, retail, hotel, and residential functions, as well as a business park and high-end automobile showroom. To the north and south of the headquarters site are developable parcels, and the bank design sets up a strong north–south visual axis through the two volumes of the building that was intended to be continued north to Manila Bay. This project essentially has two front doors: the symbolic and more formal door facing Roxas Boulevard to the south, and the functional entry along Central Boulevard on the west.

A single oval roof hovers over the two office volumes, one curved and the other rectilinear. In addition to creating a visual axis, splitting the building into two volumes connected above the second floor and elevating a portion of the building allows air to flow through, around and under the building. With the addition of a large pond and extensive landscaping, this creates a microclimate of cool air at the ground level. Roof terraces and gardens partially shaded by the oval roof soften the building and underscore the relationship between the humanmade and natural.

1

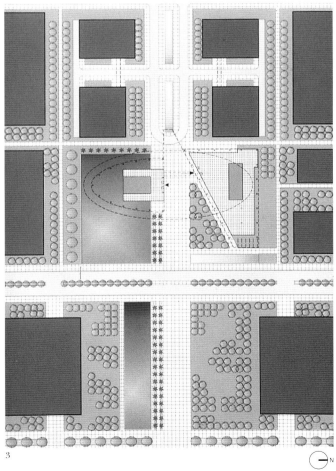

1   Perspective view from east
2   Sketch
3   Site plan

Espirito Santo Bank Competition

Design/Completion 1998
Miami, Florida
Espirito Santo Bank
440,000 square feet
Steel structure
Stainless steel panel, porcelain panel & curtainwall, stone

This proposal, for one of Portugal's oldest banking companies, takes advantage of the mixed-use program to create a building that is both dynamic and stable, expressive of the progressive yet established client. Consisting primarily of general office space on the lower floors, the building also contains retail space at ground level, and hotel/condominium functions in the curved volume that extends above the offices. Executive office suites occupy the top of the building. Due to the complexities of the program, the building has three main entries: a residential entry and a general office entry to the north, and the main bank lobby entry to the west, facing a large public plaza with reflecting pool and palm trees.

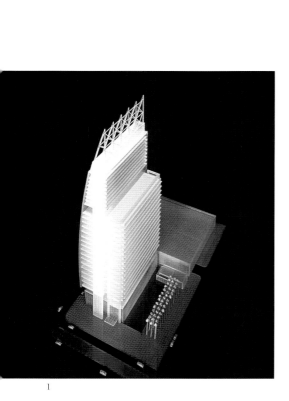

1

2

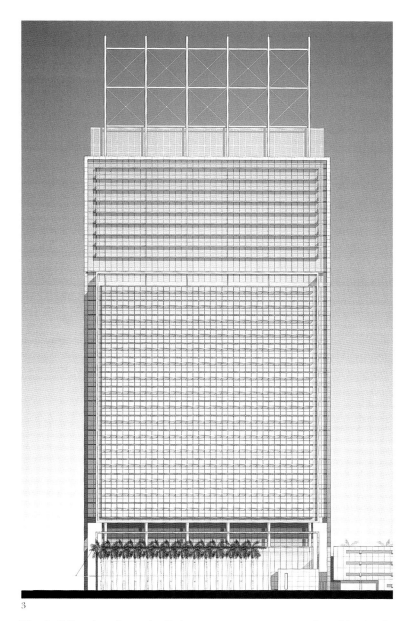

3

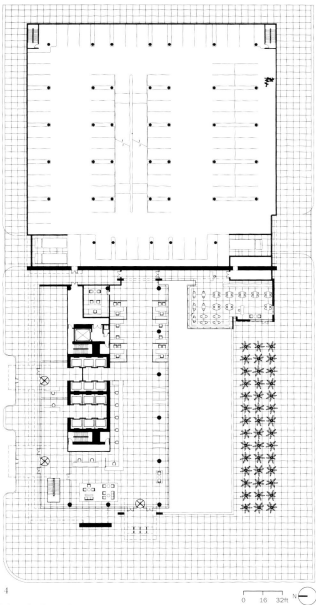

4

The building is split vertically into two volumes anchored by a solid stone band. The dynamic curved-glass element floats above the glass lobby below. A rectangular box houses the bank and office space, and on top an outdoor terrace and pool connected to a health club. The use of materials—curtainwall and stainless steel panel on the curved portion, porcelain panel and curtainwall on the rectangular box, and stone on the frame and bank lobby—reinforce the play between dynamic and stable portions of the building. Overt and suggestive imagery are employed in the form of the design. At the peak of the tower, vertical masts evoke nautical imagery, specifically relating to the history of Portuguese trading, and the general upward sweep of the form suggests motion, dynamism, and optimism.

LG Bundang Research and Development Complex

Design/Completion 1998
Bundang, Korea
LG Group
21,221 square meters
Steel structure
Glass, granite, metal

The LG Bundang Research and Development Complex was designed to be the principal research facility for the LG Group, one of the leading companies in Korea.

The site is situated on two adjacent parcels in Bundang, a new community south of Seoul and part of the greater Seoul Metropolitan area. The site is one of the more prominent in the area, bounded by two wide streets and situated at the end of a major diagonal street which leads to Seoul. Areas to the east and north will remain open or are lower developments, ensuring continued visibility. The site consists of two parcels of differing size and height restrictions, separated by a required pedestrian access.

The design for facility is comprised of two 25-story, flexible office/laboratory towers on the larger site, and a connected 10-story office building on the smaller site to the south. The buildings meet the height limits imposed on each parcel, and their positions frame the garden at the northeast corner, which can be seen from the diagonal approach from the city. The decision to provide two towers was both practical and symbolic. The twin-tower scheme allows for phasing of construction and visually divides the bulk of the building. It also reinforces the image of twins, which is prevalent in LG's corporate history, as the company was founded by two families. Between the two towers a 10-story glass reception atrium is the formal entry into the complex, a dynamic space with bridge connections between the towers. Parking and a range of amenities, including a fitness center, cafeteria, and 500-seat auditorium, are located below grade.

1

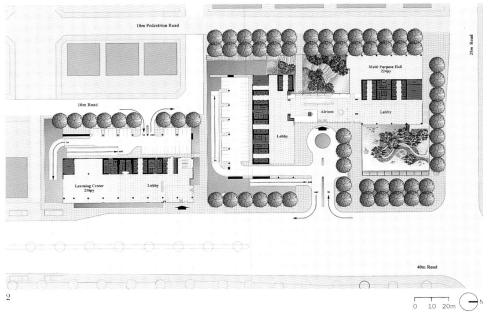

2

1   Model view from northeast
2   Site plan
3   Entrance perspective, view from the northeast
4   Atrium

3

4

CIRD Headquarters

Design/Completion 1998/ 2002
Cairo, Egypt
CIRD
700,000 square feet
Concrete structure
Local Egyptian stone

This new office complex will be located on the western bank of the Nile River, on a site that affords views of the Nile and downtown Cairo to the south. In addition to the unique opportunities of the site, municipal building restrictions, regional environmental conditions, and response to traditional precedents are the primary factors informing this design.

The complex is composed of two main building masses oriented perpendicular to the Nile and connected along the Nile Road entrance to the west. Required setbacks and height restrictions necessitated this dense, compact massing in order to maximize building area. From west to east, the spatial sequence leads from the 2-story entrance between the curved and rectilinear masses to a 4-story atrium with palm trees and a watercourse extending toward the courtyard. The courtyard, derived from the traditional Islamic type, provides a shaded and protected center to the complex. From here the view expands as the courtyard terraces down to the Nile and the curved tower sweeps north to reveal the expanse of the river. The eastern return leg of the lower building frames the river through a monumentally scaled gateway on the east–west axis.

While maximizing views, the exterior façades are also designed to respond to climatic conditions. The western, southern and eastern exposures incorporate both horizontal screens and deep ribbon windows to reduce glare and heat gain. Transoms above the screens have tinted glazing for additional solar protection. The response to solar conditions, together with variations in curtainwall treatment, adds a layer of detail and scale to the compact building mass.

1

1 Exterior view from the Nile River
2 View of atrium towards Nile
3 Ground floor plan
4 Site plan

2

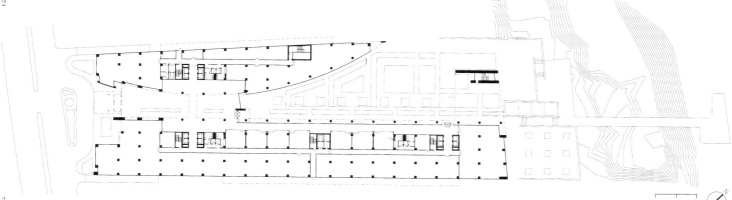

3

0   30   60ft

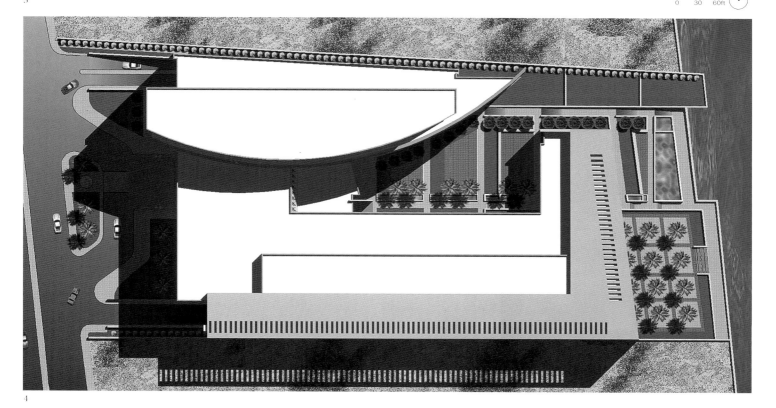

4

Crate & Barrel Corporate Headquarters

Design/Completion 2000/2001
Northbrook, Illinois
Crate & Barrel
165,000 square feet
Steel frame and exposed steel structure
Brick, glass, metal paneling

For its new corporate headquarters, Crate & Barrel wanted a classic, modern design in keeping with the aesthetic of its houseware and furniture products. This new facility, located on a 24-acre, partially wooded site north of Chicago, will include offices and merchandising spaces for review of sample products.

The building is essentially a linear bar with projecting office wings to one side. The building's siting and extensive use of glass and courtyards opens the interior to the landscape and takes advantage of the site's terrain and mature woods. A curved roof cantilevered from central columns celebrates the second-floor merchandising hall, the symbolic center of the company; the effect is of a roof that floats above the masonry walls which enclose the office areas and extending out of the building volume to define courtyards. The large-scale curve forms a backdrop for the office wings and courtyards between. Projecting into the landscape from the end of each office wing, a cantilevered glass bay houses the offices of the company's leadership.

1

2

1   Aerial view from east
2   View from southeast
3   View from southwest
4   Atrium
5   Entry level floor plan

176

3

4

5

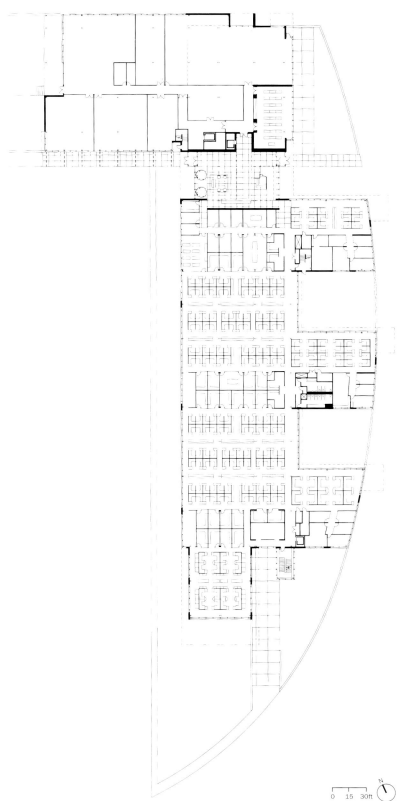

Civic

Orland Park Village Center

Design/Completion 1987/1989
Orland Park, Illinois
Village of Orland Park, Illinois
87,450 square feet
Steel, concrete
Brick, aluminum storefront and curtainwall

The Orland Park Village Center replaces the existing commercial strip as the symbolic center of this southwestern suburb of Chicago. Access to the complex is from a new road that runs perpendicular to the shopping strip, which is the village's main artery. Arranged around a rectangular green, the village hall and exhibition hall establish a formal sense of place and arrival. More informal interaction occurs along the edge of the retention pond carved into the landscape behind this space. An outdoor amphitheater and covered walkway link the village hall and exhibition building with the new recreation center, and provide a public gathering place along the water's edge.

Continued

1

2

3

4

1   Western view of village center
2   Exhibition hall
3   North view of village hall
4   Axonometric
Opposite:
    Main entrance of village hall

180

In order to unite the disparate elements, a vocabulary of formal types related to function was developed; these forms repeat in each of the three buildings, with adjustments to particular siting conditions. Assembly spaces have bowed roofs, meeting rooms are cylindrical pavilions, and lobbies and public circulation are expressed as columned halls. The village hall is the focal point of the complex, and its hierarchical importance is underscored by its symmetrical composition—it is the only symmetrical building on the site—and by the use of formal elements unique to the complex. Its massing and placement resolve the axes of the entry road and the green.

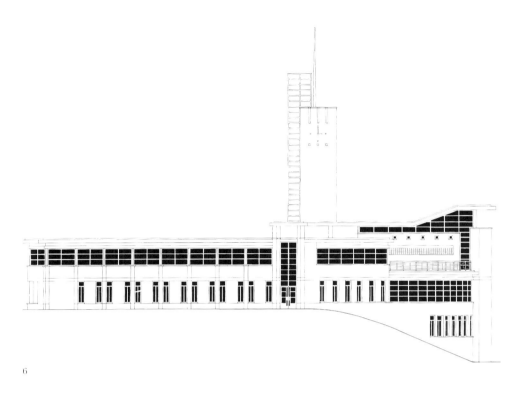

6

7

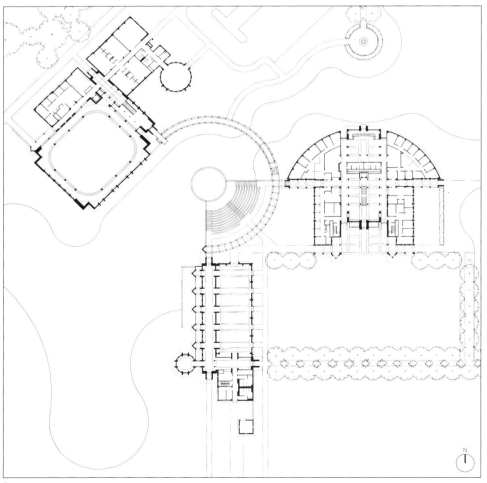

8

Arcade   Pavilion   Linear Columnar Gallery   Loft   Clear Span hall   Singular Symbolic Form

9

10

International Terminal, O'Hare International Airport

Design/Completion 1989/1993
Chicago, Illinois
City of Chicago, Department of Aviation & Department of Public Works
1,125,000 square feet
Steel structure
Metal panel, glass

Sited at the entrance to O'Hare Airport and clearly visible from the freeway, the 800-foot long arc of the International Terminal's ticketing pavilion creates a new image for the complex, at a scale appropriate to the highway and the airplane. The gently arcing form recalls a bridge or an aircraft wing with its smooth, taut exterior and skeletal interior. The 21-gate terminal handles all foreign airline departures and all international arrivals, with departures on the upper level, arrivals on the lower level, and baggage handling and support spaces at the mid-level on grade.

The embodiment of movement, both of pedestrians and aircraft, inspires the building's overall organization as well as its details. A linear, hierarchical sequence of discrete spaces enhances the sense of movement and transition for both arriving and departing passengers. From the ticketing pavilion on the upper level, a broad corridor lined with concessions leads west to a central security checkpoint and to the boarding concourse wings.

Continued

1

2

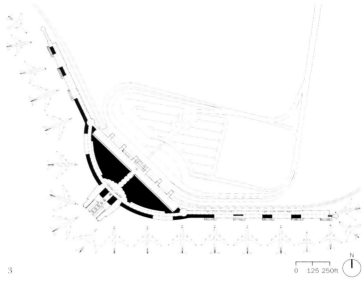

3

4

1   View of control tower
2   Dusk view of International terminal
3   Upper level plan
4   View from tarmac

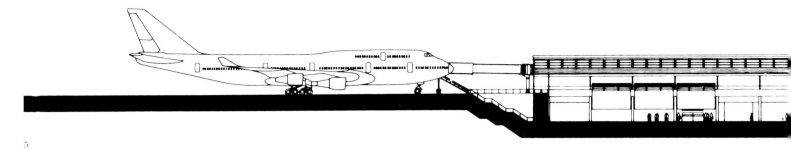

5

Ceiling planes along this sequence float independently from the exposed structure, describing sinuous shapes that heighten the sense of movement. Three shed-like forms at mid-level on the freeway side enclose the people-mover station linking the terminal to the rest of the airport, and can be reached from either the arrivals or departure level. The control tower on the runway side is a visible vertical fulcrum for both the interior and exterior composition. In form and detail, the building celebrates the idea of flight, and creates a memorable experience for the traveler.

6

7

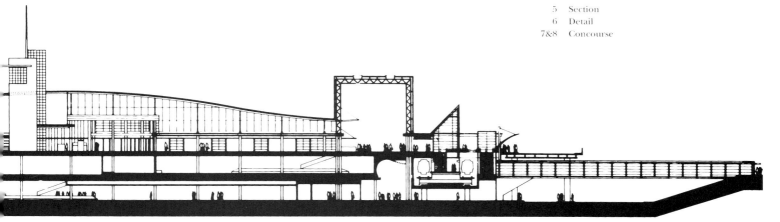

8

Chek Lap Kok Airport Competition

Design/Completion 1992
Hong Kong
Hong Kong Provisional Airport Authority
5,380,000 square feet
Steel, concrete
Glass, metal panel

The site for this new airport is on an artificially created strip of land along the water, with limited buildable area. This design combines satellite and direct contact concourses with a total of 120 gates, integrates a rail line and automobile traffic, and provides parking, hotel and commercial areas. A vocabulary of long, streamlined bars unifies the composition, and expresses movement of people, aircraft, baggage, and transit. Architectural form and volume provide visual cues to direct people naturally through the terminal complex. The check-in hall, a grand public space with a soaring vaulted ceiling, corresponds to the concentration of movement to the center of the terminal and on toward the gates. Circular nodes at vertical circulation unify streamlined and elongated forms, and orient passengers. The curved lines of the roof again suggest movement, and ground the forms onto the site.

1

2

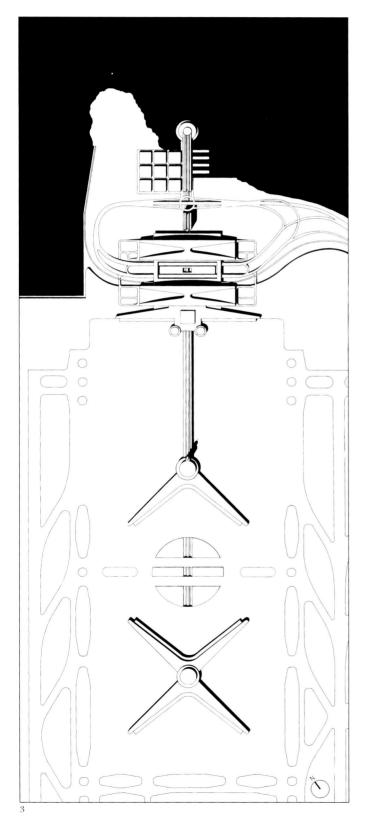

3

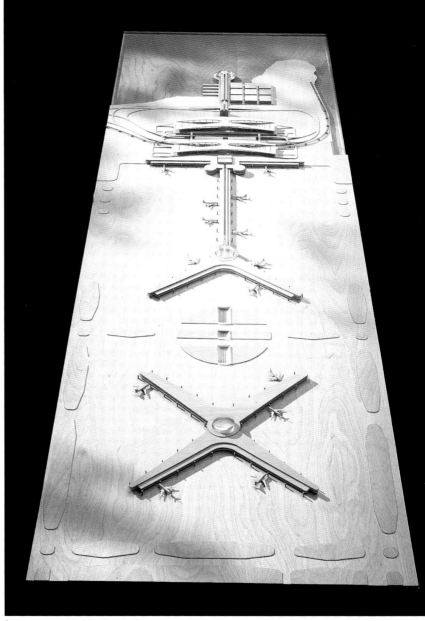

4

1 Sketch, interior view of terminal
2 Aerial view from southwest
3 Site plan
4 Model, aerial view from southwest

Peggy Notebaert Nature Center

Design/Completion 1995/1999
Chicago, Illinois
Chicago Academy of Sciences
73,000 square feet
Fabricated, structural steel with composite floor deck, concrete footings
and basement walls
Weathered-edge rustic fieldstone, exterior insulation finish system,
glazed aluminum curtainwall system

The Peggy Notebaert Nature Museum is the new home of the Chicago Academy of Sciences, which had been housed since 1893 in a neoclassical building one-half mile south in Lincoln Park. The Academy's mission, to make accessible the natural history of the Midwest, is evident both physically and metaphorically in the new museum's siting, form and materials. The design emphasizes the connection and interdependence of the natural and human-made environments, illustrated by the use of the history of its park setting. The angular masses that house the exhibits recall the shifting sand dunes that existed on the site before it was converted to park in the late 19th century. They also suggest an abstraction of geological layers, similar to Alfred Caldwell's interpretation of the formation of the Midwest in the Rookery across the street. The indeterminate quality of these angular masses also expresses the dynamics of nature.

1

1 Section looking east
2 View of main entrance approach
3 Entry level plan
4 View from the southwest

2

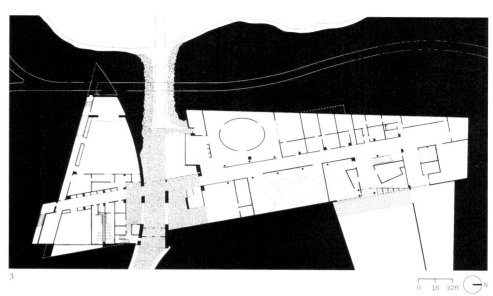

3

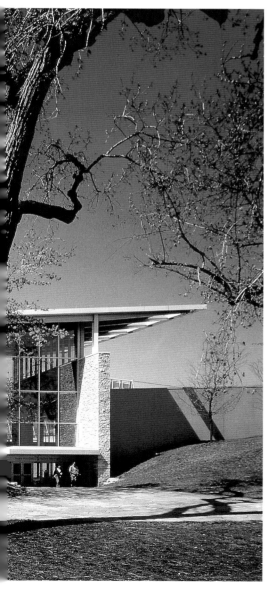

4

The building is embedded in the site and, at its peak, the roof hovers just below the tree line. The placement of the new museum was determined by the footprint of the park maintenance sheds that formerly occupied the site and, in respecting that footprint, the existing trees and contours were able to be preserved.

Entry to the museum is through an incision in the landscape—a section through the site that creates a gateway to the pond from the entrance and emphasizes the building's integral relationship with the site. A natural stone wall, and stone paving mark the entry to the transparent lobby. Beyond the lobby, a ravine with native plants physically and visually connects the museum to the pond. The glazed butterfly haven, featuring Midwest species, looks onto this space as well. At various points throughout the museum's exhibit space, exterior views connect what is outside to what is being explained inside.

5

5   Section through lobby
6   View looking northeast of birdwalk and butterfly haven
7   View from the west

6

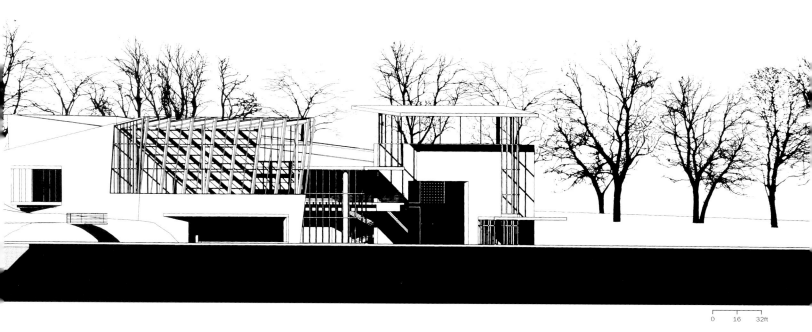

9

On the second floor, a terrace connects to the bird walk that extends to the trees along the edge of the pond. The new landscape design, which can be experienced from inside and outside, recreates several natural communities around the building, from pond to woodland slope, to native prairie on the south-facing slope. The museum is an educational tool, and is a metaphor for the relationship between human and nature.

10

8   Aerial view of museum looking north
9   View of outdoor dining terrace
10   View facing south of birdwalk with downtown
     Chicago in background

11

12

13

14

YMCA – Centennial Place

Design/Completion 1997/1998
Atlanta, Georgia
YMCA
25,000 square feet
Rolled steel trusses, bar-joist, light-frame steel construction, and concrete block
Galvanized roofing, metal siding, stucco finish, storefront assembly with aluminum sunscreens

This community center is a gym and activities center for the adjoining elementary school, as well as a daycare, health facility, adult education, and career development center for the people who live and work in the area.

The client's mission recalls the social optimism of the century's early Modernists, in its desire to use building to revitalize a neglected urban area. The site borders four distinct communities—corporate, academic, civic, and residential—and it was the ideal interaction of these four constituents that generated the cruciform organization of the building plan. The facility responds to the inner-city site complexity with muscular sectional variation and rich color, and sustains this vigor through the interior. Eroded corners and apparent deflecting of loads lighten the overall massing. The building takes advantage of its sloping site by providing a lower, more private entrance for the school, and upper-level entries for the community. The building itself, being in a prominent location, acts as a focal point in the area, and this is reinforced by a skylight above the climbing wall that acts as a beacon for the community.

1

2

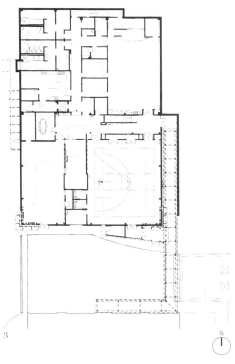

3

4

St Mark's Catholic Church Competition

Design/Completion 1999
Miami, Florida
Archdiocese of Miami
25,000 square feet (seats up to 1200)
Concrete, glulam wood beams
Concrete, wood, stained-glass, high impact curtainwall skin, slate floors

The competition design for St Mark's Catholic Church proposes a single, soaring roof structure of laminated wood beams, supported on four concrete columns, which floats above the enclosing walls of the church. The roof curves gently upward from the entrance to the eastern altar, allowing morning light to flow through the large expanses of stained glass which drape the surfaces behind the altar. From the chapel behind the altar, one can enter the walled garden behind the church. The chapel, reconciliation rooms, and baptistery engage the exterior walls but retain a quality of precious objects sheltered below the floating roof above. The western entry wall of the church is constructed entirely of operable walls, in order to allow the congregation to flow out into the main plaza of the school campus of which the church is a part.

1

2

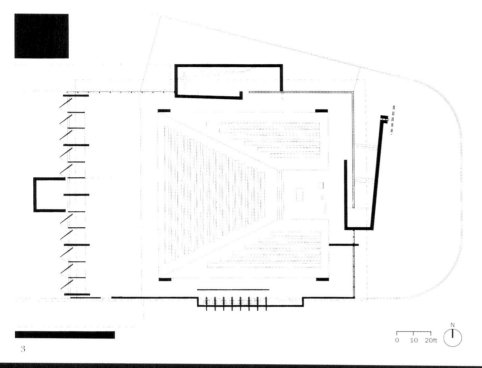

1&2   Interior view of Church
  3   Floor plan
  4   Model view

0   10   20ft   N

3

4

Miami Beach Regional Library Competition

Design/Completion 1997
Miami Beach, Florida
City of Miami Beach
40,000 square feet
Steel joists and columns
Keystone (local stone), high-impact curtainwall skin

This competition was for a library that is part of a new arts center developed around Collins park. The arts center also includes the refurbished library, now museum, by Arata Isozaki, a rehearsal facility for the Miami City Ballet by Architectonica, and a new parking structure. The ballet and parking are on the block just to the west of the library site. The entrance to the library faces the restored park.

The dynamic roof arcs towards the park and the library's highly visible main entrance. Connected to the library and designed to operate as a stand-alone unit, a coffee shop and auditorium can be open during and after library hours. Coffee-shop tables spill onto the sidewalk, creating an animated streetscape in the cultural campus.

Luminous sails of light describe the pavilion-like space of the reading room. Designed to maximize controlled natural light, the library is conceived of, in the words of Labrouste, as an "open book". Clear in its use and layout, the library attempts to recapture the sense of space historically associated with library design, while providing a solution that is efficient and economical to operate, memorable and fun to use, and brimming with the excitement and optimism typical of Miami Beach architecture.

1

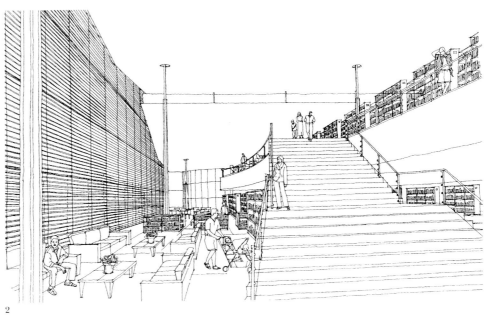
2

1　Entry perspective
2　Interior perspective
3　Ground floor plan
4　Aerial view

John G. Shedd Aquarium

Design/Completion 1999/multiple-phase completion dates
Chicago, Illinois
John G. Shedd Aquarium
55,000 square feet
Concrete structure
Georgia marble—exterior; Tennessee Gray floors, fossil stone,
glass mosaic tiles, terracotta interior

Perkins & Will is part of a team creating a master plan for a phased expansion of the John G. Shedd Aquarium. The expansion, which will be realized over the next ten years, will include five new thematic exhibits, and renovations and upgrades to the existing structural and mechanical systems. The design respects the historic significance of the original 1927 landmark building while also providing state-of-the-art exhibition space.

Restoration of the central rotunda, remodeling and expansion of the gift shop, restoration of the Caribbean Reef tank, and a surrounding multi-media exhibit are complete. Subsequent phases will include the creation of geographically oriented and interactive exhibits that focus on the Amazon River, the Philippines, and the Great Lakes. The Amazon exhibit will combine two existing galleries and will open husbandry areas to public view. The Philippine Islands exhibit, centered on a 350,000-gallon shark tank, will be at terrace level and also below grade, in order to preserve the integrity of the beaux-arts exterior. The Great Lakes exhibit will also be at terrace level, with views to Lake Michigan.

1

2

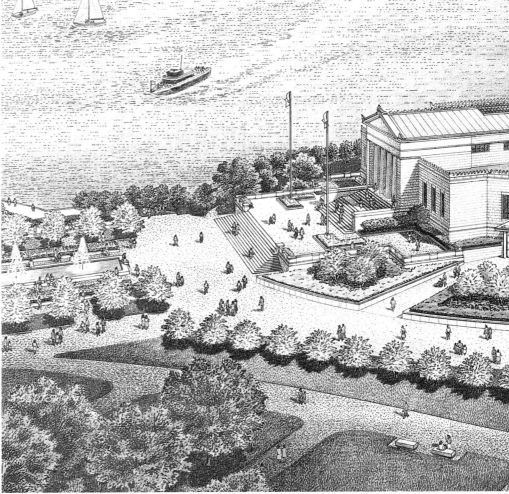

3

1 Rotunda during dive exhibit
2 Renovated Caribbean reef tank in restored rotunda
3 View from southwest
4 Cutaway showing exhibit renovation and building expansion

4

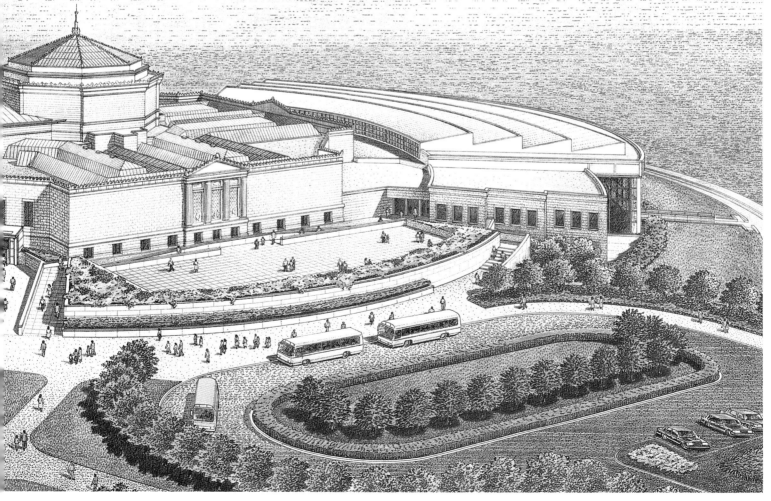

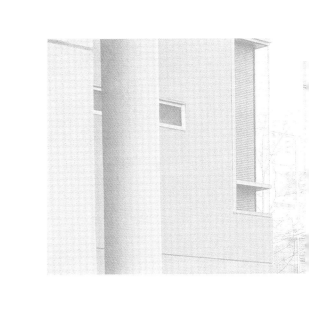

Housing

Katherine and William Mayer Residences, Tulane University

Design/Completion 1995/1997
New Orleans, Louisiana
Tulane University
95,000 square feet
Concrete structure
Brick, stucco, anodized aluminum-framed windows, glass block, metal sun screens

This 256-bed, student housing project uses collage as a strategy to resolve a critical intersection in the campus plan, and to create an architecture appropriate to its New Orleans and Tulane University setting. The site is located at an important spatial and stylistic intersection in the campus plan: the intersection of the traditional Newcomb Quadrangle and McAlister Street, which is the main student activity spine with its modern buildings. The project provides critical edge-definition in the campus plan, and its architectural expression forms an aesthetic bridge between the two axes. In addition, its layered façades and internal, shaded courtyards respond to the housing traditions of New Orleans.

A common modern-housing prototype, the double-loaded perimeter block is modified with additions and subtractions to create hierarchy, spatial transparency, and layering. Eight residential units are grouped to form a hierarchy of public, semi-public, and private interior and exterior spaces. The resulting design provides a strong sense of community for its residents, centered on the main exterior courtyard, which unifies the scheme.

1

2

3

1 View from east
2 View from south
3 East façade
4 Axonometric
5 Exploded axonometric
6 South facade

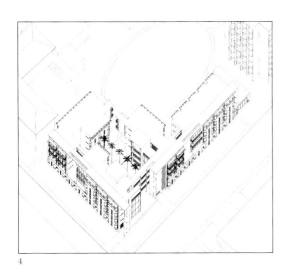

4

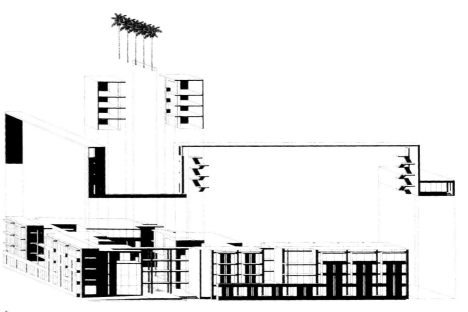

5

6

8

9

10

Opposite:
　　　View of courtyard
　8　West elevation, section
9&10　Laundry terrace

11   Second floor plan
12   First floor plan
13   Recreational lobby

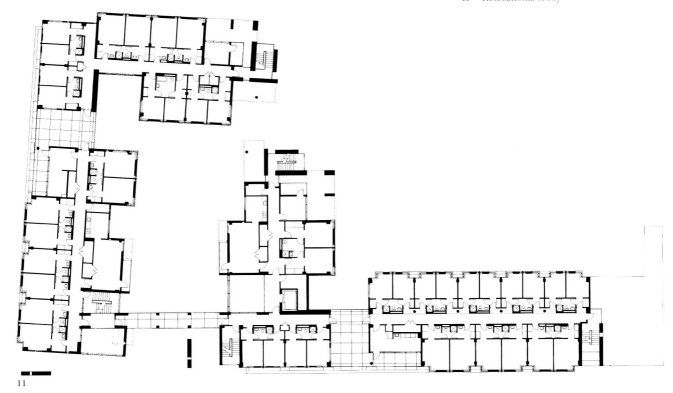

11

12

0   8   16ft   N

212

EXIT

13

Nara Towers and Marina

Design/Completion 1997
Beirut, Lebanon
Hardco
100,000 square meters; 18,000 square meters underground parking
Reinforced concrete structure
Stone, glass

The Nara Towers hotel and Marina is located on a triangular site formed by the divergence of the main coastal road, the "Corniche," from the seaside. The 48-story high-rise, and 9-story low-rise hotel towers afford exceptional views of the Mediterranean Sea. The complex also includes restaurants, a health club, meeting rooms, a ballroom, retail space, and public congregation spaces, as well as outdoor gardens, pools and terraces, arcades, and shoreline promenades.

The overall organization of the complex is suggested by the site. The high-rise follows the straight edge of the coastal road, and the low-rise which intersects it follows the edge of the sea. Entry from the Corniche is through a 6-story glass atrium connecting the two towers. The curve of the low-rise continues into the sea in the form of the breakwater, which encloses the marina. To the north and south are public beaches. Private cabanas extending from the low-rise front the southern beach, and terminate at a public plaza and restaurant at the midpoint of the marina. After years of internal conflict in the country, this project is symbolic of Beirut's rebirth, and its optimism about the future.

1   Elevation
2   Model, view from south
3   Main entry level
4   Model, view from north
5   Site plan

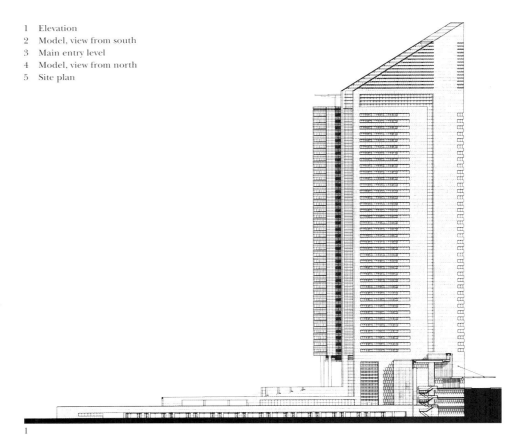

1

2

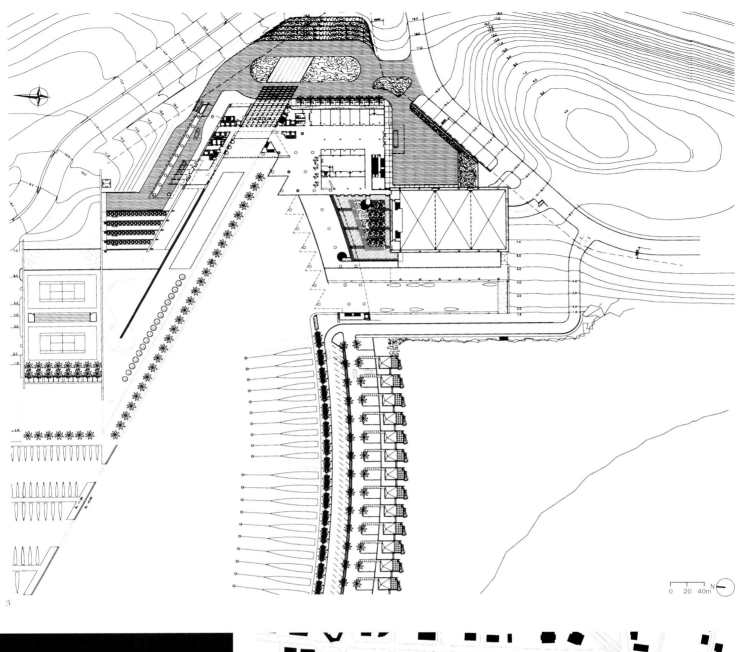

3

4

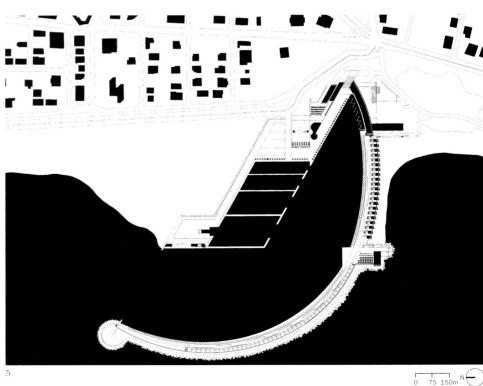

5

Ain El-Mreisseh Hotel and Marina

Design/Completion 1998
Beirut, Lebanon
Confidential client
450,000 square feet
Concrete structure
Steel, glass, granite

The proposal for the Ain El-Mreisseh Hotel and Marina is for a site located along Beirut's Corniche Road. From this site there are dramatic views of the Mediterranean Sea, and the Lebanese mountains. In the design proposal, interlocking residential and hotel towers rest on a 4-story base containing separate entrance lobbies for hotel, residential and retail, and services such as function rooms, retail and restaurants, pool, and health club. Below grade is access to the Marina and restaurant across the Corniche, and additional retail and parking.

Above the podium level there is a horizontal separation, expressed as a void, between the hotel and residential towers. The low glass residential tower penetrates the hotel slab, which continues above the residential tower after a 2-story gap. Differentiation of material—glass residential tower and stone hotel—accentuates the effect of interlocking, separate volumes. The curve of the single-loaded hotel slab gives it a presence on the street, and focuses on views to the north and northeast. The hotel service core disengages itself behind the clean sweep of the curve, and recreation areas and support functions are located to the rear of the site.

1

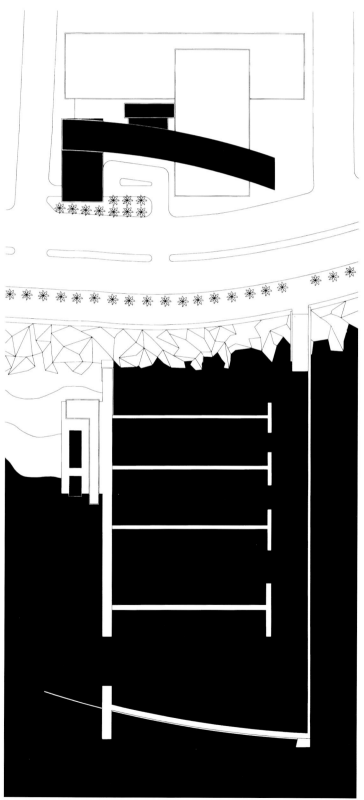

1   View from south
2   Site plan
3   View from south

Skybridge at One North Halsted

Design/Completion 1998/2001
Chicago, Illinois
Dearborn Development
780,000 square feet, 237 units
Concrete structure
Concrete, and glass exterior

This project consists of a 39-story condominium tower resting on a 4-story base of retail space and parking. The site is located west of downtown Chicago, between two north–south arteries of very different character. To the east of the site is an 8-lane expressway which demarcates the current boundary of the high-rises west of the loop. To the west is a section of Halsted Street known as "Greektown," which consists of 3- to 4-story retail and restaurant entertainment buildings.

The design is a base-and-tower scheme which reinforces these two urban conditions. A 39-story linear housing slab parallels the expressway on the eastern portion of the site, to maximize views of the Chicago skyline from the residential units. The mass of the tower is an urban marker defining the canyon created by the depressed expressway and marking the western edge of the downtown. The 4-story base is a transitional element, consistent with the scale of buildings along Halsted Street.

The building's design challenges the typical residential tower model, in order to accommodate flexibility and variety of unit options, and to humanize the scale of the tower. The manipulation of mass and void, opacity, and transparency creates a random, ad hoc village-like quality, as opposed to the monolithic vertical slab of most current high-rise residential design. A large transparent opening, spanned by glass bridges, forms an over-scaled urban window, and also suggests an alternate reading of the building as two interconnected towers rather than a single, large mass.

Planning of the typical floor provides options, variety, and flexibility to prospective buyers. Each floor has six different layouts for both one and two-bedroom units, and unit sizes are alternated in plan to maximize possible combinations. A variety of exterior extensions—projections, recesses or terraces—can be glazed in without compromising the integrity of the building's design. This is possible because of the built-in, random quality of the exterior.

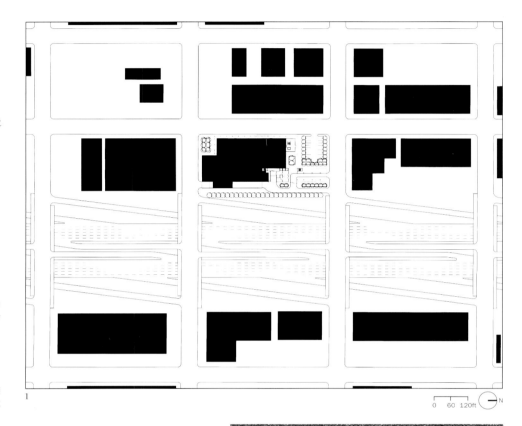

1

0   60 120ft   N

1   Site plan
2   Sketch
Opposite:
    View from east

2

218

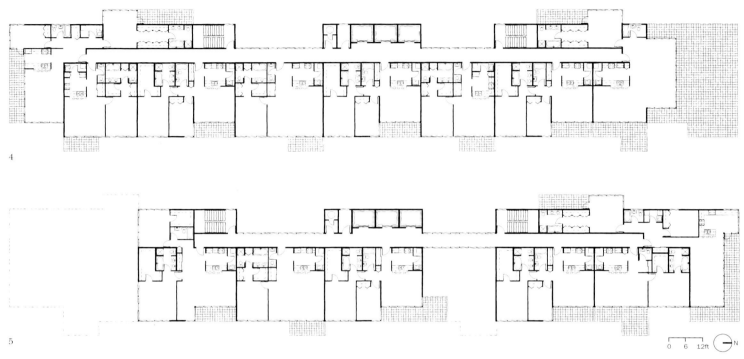

4

5

0 6 12ft   N

6

7

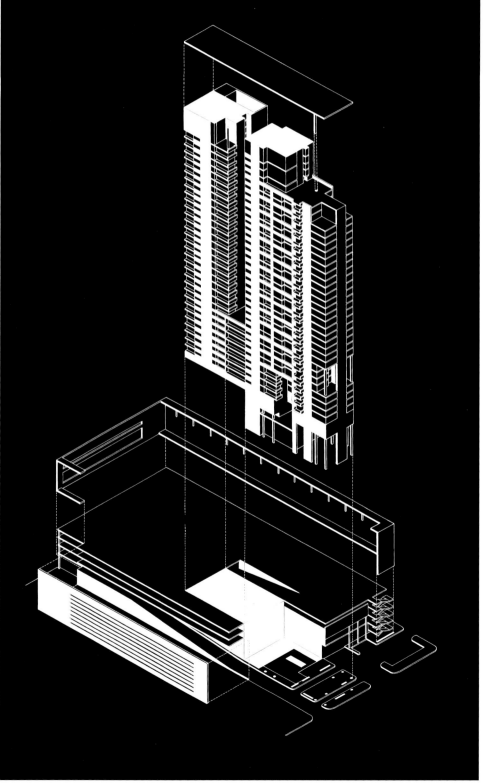

8

Interiors

A.T. Kearney

Design/Completion 1991/1992
Chicago, Illinois
A.T. Kearney
130,000 square feet
Slate wall panels, lacquer, painted drywall, glass, terrazzo flooring, carpet

The consulting firm of A.T. Kearney Inc. occupies four floors in the USG Building in downtown Chicago. The design of the headquarters reflects the diverse management approaches the firm explores and advocates for its clients. Consultant work areas consist of dispersed, shared team working areas, and dedicated "personal harbor" workstations. Extensive use of glass in all offices, conference rooms, and training rooms creates a sense of openness and transparency. In the work areas, simple materials in their natural states—cherry wall panels, black granite tables, leather upholsteries—contrast with cleft slate wall panels, terrazzo floors, stainless steel and bronze detailing, and precast concrete in the public areas, providing a variety of experience, texture, light, and form. In contrast to the more neutral palette of the offices, the reception desk and 4-story staircase become functional sculpture, distinguished by their forms and materials as centers of activity.

1

1 View of conferencing from atrium
2 Reception
3 24th floor plan
4 View of atrium
5 Detail at reception desk

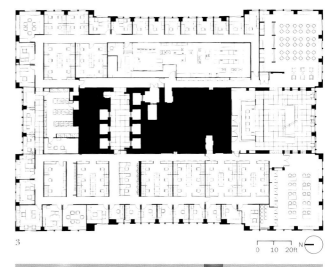

2

3

0 10 20ft   N

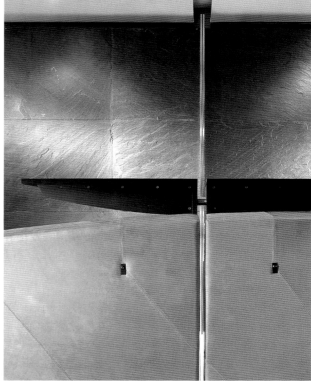

4

5

Martin/Williams Advertising and FAME

Design/Completion 1993/1994
Minneapolis, Minnesota
Martin/Williams Inc.
72,000 square feet

Glass bridge openings and a multi-floor stairway unify distinct yet connected areas of the environment created for this nationally recognized advertising firm. Through the use of materials native to the Midwest, the design is at once simultaneously rooted in its location, yet also transcends the particular. Innovations include a full-scale climbing wall that penetrates two floors, creating a metaphor of focused goals and achievement, and wide, angular corridors that occasionally meet with the office tower's glass curtainwall to provide an expansive view of the surrounding downtown skyline. Creatively displayed, state-of-the-art technology provides a means for Martin/Williams to display its own work.

The floor devoted to its subsidiary company, FAME, offers its own distinct personality, with a deconstructed look. The moody and theatrical design utilizes exposed framing, brick walls, and concrete floors, in keeping with the retail focus common among the four sister companies.

1

2

3

226

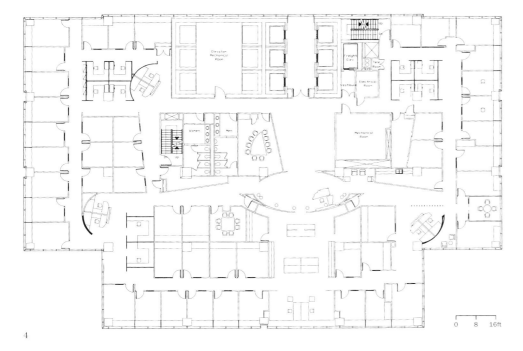

1 FAME coordinator position
2 Martin/Williams lobby, 28th floor
3 FAME elevator lobby
4 FAME 26th floor plan
5 Martin/Williams conference room
6 Martin/Williams lobby, 28th floor

4

5

6

Fallon McElligott, 29th Floor Expansion

Design/Completion 1995/ 1996
Minneapolis, Minnesota
Fallon McElligott
52,000 square feet

The advertising firm Fallon McElligott wanted its new offices, located on the seventh and most recently completed floor designed by Perkins & Will in this building, to be on the leading edge of creativity and innovation. The client stressed the need for a flexible environment that captured the energy of its "hot shop" reputation. Inter-office communications, workstation flexibility, and an environment that supports the creative energy of the entire staff were important elements in the overall design of this "virtual office". The raw office space, with upward and outward sloping glass walls, offered dramatic and dizzying vistas that provided an immediate, "on-the-edge" feel. The new design for the interior combines those vistas with forced changes of perspective, and the creative use of space and materials. A conical staircase, wrapped in warm-hued cherry and Australian lacewood, creates a curved avenue to the firm's three floors. Similar woods and a natural color palette are carried throughout the office.

In keeping with the firm's culture of openness and equality, private offices are of equal size, with no doors.

The design also builds upon the evolving concept of teaming and flexibility. Workstations are a series of birch veneer panels supported by hot, rolled-steel "boots". These mobile work cabinets became representative of the alternative work environment. Wheeled around with the individual, employees simply "dock" computers into these custom cabinets and hook up their computer telephone and other equipment using single connective devices. The office gathering place is a 1950s-style diner, complete with soda fountain.

1

2

3

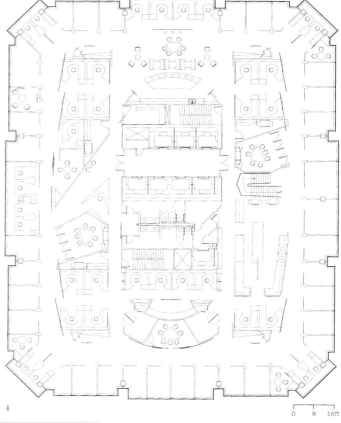

4

0 8 16ft

5

Towers Perrin, Stamford

Design/Completion 1997/1999
Stamford, Connecticut
Towers Perrin
61,500 square feet on four floors
Wood paneling and custom furniture—pear-stained maple, black granite
panels and St. Croix limestone tile in elevator lobby

The corporate headquarters for Towers
Perrin in Stamford, Connecticut is the
fourth project undertaken for this client
by Perkins & Will. The design of the space
makes tangible the company Chairman's
egalitarian management style. There is
one size for offices and one size for
workstations used throughout, and the
customer-contact spaces, reception, and
conference rooms are spacious and
comfortable. The space maximizes the
available ceiling height, and vertical baffles
screen the multiple conference rooms
from unwanted distractions. Light
carpeting and wall finishes contrast
dramatically with dark, midnight blue
accents, and the judicious use of fine
materials.

1

2

3

4

1 Sixth floor plan
2 Typical 'one size fits all' private office
3 View into conference room
4 Reception/conference room break-out space

Northwestern Medical Faculty Foundation

Design/Completion 1997/1999
Chicago, Illinois
Northwestern Medical Faculty Foundation (NMFF)
270,000 square feet
Wood, drywall canopies, indirect lighting

Twenty-one clinical practice groups, including Obstetrics, Gynecology, Plastic Surgery, Ophthalmology, and General Medicine, have been relocated from various buildings on the Northwestern Medical Campus to seven floors of the Galter Pavilion. The design for these new spaces balances the need for cohesive space with the desire for each practice group to have an individual identity. NMFF also desired its own distinctive identity within the hospital, while maintaining overall consistency of design language and image.

Consistent design in the interior and the selection of furniture visually links the practice groups within the NMFF, while varied color palettes create distinctions between the functions. Primary circulation encircles each floor, keeping the environment familiar, and comfortable to navigate. Varied materials, floor patterns, and signage direct patients to their destinations. In order to accommodate a dense program within limited space, the patient waiting area for each floor serves several practices. A circular station guides patients from the waiting area to individual reception areas for each practice group.

1

1 Reception and patient waiting area
2 Typical floor elevator lobby
3 Typical nurses station and guest phone booth
4 Detail at patient waiting area
5 14th floor plan

2

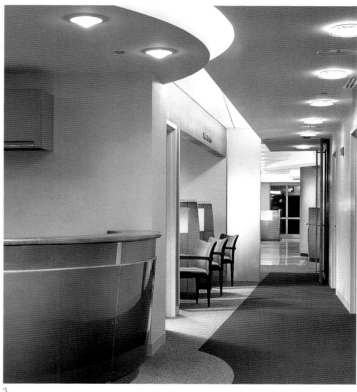

3

4

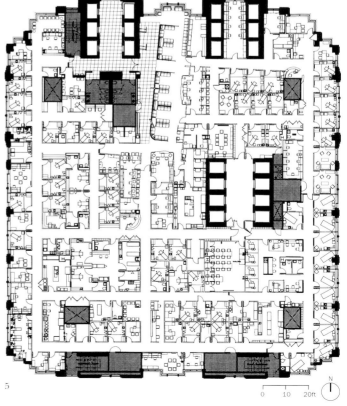

5

0   10   20ft

American Hospital Association

Design/Completion 1998/1999
Chicago, Illinois
American Hospital Association
38,000 square feet
Glazed porcelain, tile flooring, painted drywall, carpet, glass,
aluminum flooring

The American Hospital Association, a non-profit health advocate association, recently relocated its three for-profit subsidiaries into its main headquarters. This project required a balance between community and privacy for all of the newly consolidated subsidiaries. The project entailed consolidation of the association's core functions, in order to vacate the two floors of the project area. An accelerated project schedule minimized work interruption, and costs were kept under control by re-using 60 percent of the existing build-out, and by re-using doors, light fixtures, and some furniture.

The new office layout combines open floor plan work areas with private offices. A single, low-profile workstation standard is used. Glass-fronted private offices incorporate natural light and views. A Cyber Café and multiple teaming areas accommodate gathering for the subsidiary companies.

1

2

3

4

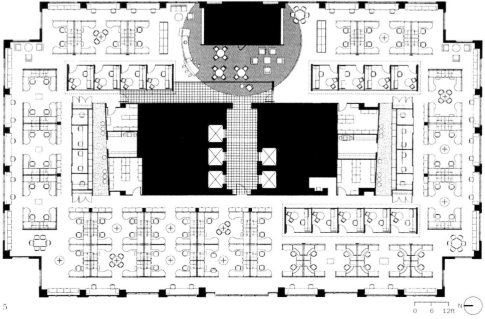

5

1   Interior guest offices
2   Reception and guest conferencing
3&4   Café and team break-out space
5   29th floor plan

0   6   12ft   N

Tribune Interactive

Design/Completion 1999/2000
Chicago, Illinois
Chicago Tribune
85,000 square feet
Glass, steel

The abandoned printing press room in the lower levels of the landmark Tribune Tower is the site for a new, open environment office space for the Chicago Tribune's Internet-based division. The new high-tech interventions will contrast existing features of the 3-story high industrial space, such as the glazed tile that covers the steel columns. Steel bridges will cut across the 3-story main room, which will be punctuated by nine glass-walled conference rooms stacked in 3-story vertical "towers". The interactive group will occupy 270 open workstations in this main space. An existing loading dock will be refitted with glass walls in order to introduce natural light into the space below. Also designed within this space are a 12,500-square-foot company fitness center, and a new corporate conference and training center, both on two levels.

1

1   View of atrium from second level
2   View of conferencing towers from first level
3   First level plan

2

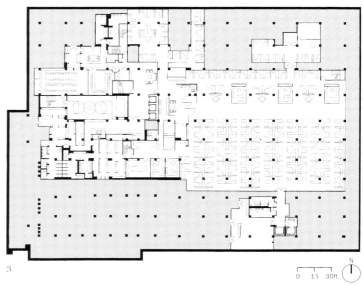

3

0 15 30ft

N

Firm Profile

Firm Profile

Perkins & Will, founded in 1935, is a professional service firm staffed with architects, interior designers, and planners. With offices in Chicago, Atlanta, Charlotte, Los Angeles, Miami, Minneapolis, New York and Paris, the firm practices internationally, and has completed projects in 49 states and 37 countries.

Perkins & Will first gained national recognition for their design of educational facilities. Since then, hundreds of school, college and university projects have been planned and designed worldwide.

In the 1950s, design of healthcare facilities became an equally significant part of the practice. Today, the firm's medical design practice has completed projects for more than 300 medical institutions in the US and overseas.

The corporate–commercial practice of Perkins & Will matured in the 1960s. The corporate practice encompasses the design of major headquarters buildings, research and development facilities, and interior environments for clients in both product and service industries. The commercial practice includes investment office buildings, hotels and conference centers, major mixed-use developments, and space-planning assignments. More than 50-million square feet of office, research, banking, retailing, and lodging space has been planned and designed in the past 10 years.

Perkins & Will is one of the nation's most respected design firms, both for its excellence in design and service to clients. Of equal importance is the firm's adherence to a design process that emphasizes commitment, communication and coordination, resulting in responsive service and projects that satisfy client goals.

Through the years, the firm has received hundreds of awards for its projects, and its principals have been honored for their contributions to their profession. The firm was recently named by the American Institute of Architects as Firm of The Year for 1999.

From a modest beginning 65 years ago, Perkins & Will has grown to become an organization of more than 300 design professionals who serve clients on a worldwide basis, with a dedication to quality that was established by our founders six decades ago . . . 'the quiet trust and satisfaction of clients and (the) public who know their interests have been thoughtfully served'.

Principals

Fereidoon Afshari	Charles Knight
Charles Alexander	John Lijewski
Eric Aukee	James Lubawy
Stuart Aynsley	Jean Mah
Kristy Barclay	Henry A. Mann
Raymond Bordwell	I. Lewis Nix
Ila Burdett	Carl Ordemann
Manuel Cadrecha	Terrence Owens
Gaylaird Christopher	David Paeper
Barbara Crum	Robert Peterson
Ted H. Davis	James Prendergast
M. Coleman DeMoss	Leslie M. Saunders
G. William Doerge	Nick Seierup
Phyllis Dubinsky-Klein	Philip A. Shive
Tama Duffy	Leonard Skiba
Michael Fejes	James H. Smith
Jocelyn Frederick	Daniel Spencer
Jose Gelabert-Navia	P. Gary Swords
David A. Hansen	Steven Turckes
Philip Harrison	William C. Viehman
Arthur Hoey	Gary Wheeler
David C. Johnson	Diedre Woodring
Jerry Johnson	James Young
Ralph E. Johnson	

Awards

1999 Architecture Firm Award
American Institute of Architects

1999 Distinguished Building Award
Mayer Residences, Tulane
University
Chicago Chapter of the American
Institute of Architects

1999 Certificate of Merit
New Albany Learning Community
Association of School Business
Officials International

1998 Interior Architecture Honor Award
Temple Hoyne Buell Hall
Chicago Chapter of the American
Institute of Architects

1998 Citation of Merit
Temple Hoyne Buell Hall
Chicago Chapter of the American
Institute of Architects

1998 Honor Award
International School of Manila
Chicago Chapter of the American
Institute of Architects

1998 Honor Award
Nagoya International School
Chicago Chapter of the American
Institute of Architects

1998 Citation of Merit
Palo Alto Middle School
Chicago Chapter of the American
Institute of Architects

1997 Thomas H. Magidan Award
Chemical and Life Sciences
Building
Illinois Capital Development Board

1997 Distinguished Building Award
Chemical and Life Sciences
Building
Chicago Chapter of the American
Institute of Architects

1997 Merit Award
North Fort Myers High School
The American School and
University

1997 Citation
South Georgia Medical Center,
Pearlman Cancer Center
Modern Healthcare

1996 Distinguished Building Award
Vernal G. Riffe, Jr. Building
Chicago Chapter of the American
Institute of Architects

1996 Corporate Design Award
Fallon McElligott
American Society of Interior
Designers, Minnesota Chapter

1996 Best Large Office Award
Fallon McElligott/Duffy, Inc.
Interiors Magazine

1996 First Place Product Design
Fallon McElligott
American Society of Interior
Designers, Minnesota Chapter

1996 Award for Excellence
South Georgia Medical Center,
Pearlman Cancer Center
Georgia Chapter of the American
Institute of Architects

1995 Distinguished Building Award
North Fort Myers High School
Chicago Chapter of the American
Institute of Architects

1995 National Honor Award
Perry Community Educational
Village
American Institute of Architects

1995 Honor Award
Vernal G. Riffe Building, Ohio
State University
Cleveland Chapter of the American
Institute of Architects

1994 National Honor Award
Troy High School
American Institute of Architects

1994 Distinguished Building Award
Perry Community Educational
Village
Chicago Chapter of the American
Institute of Architects

1993 Distinguished Building Award
International Terminal at O'Hare
International Airport
Chicago Chapter of the American
Institute of Architects

1993 The Divine Detail Award
International Terminal at O'Hare
International Airport
Chicago Chapter of the American
Institute of Architects

1993 Interior Architecture Award
International Terminal at O'Hare
International Airport
Chicago Chapter of the American
Institute of Architects

1993 Interior Architecture Award
Offices of Perkins & Will
Chicago Chapter of the American
Institute of Architects

1993 Citation
Perry Community Education Village
The American School and
University

1993 The Crow Island School Citation
Perry Community Education Village
The American School and
University

1993 The Shirley Cooper Award
Perry Community Education Village
American Association of School
Administrators and the American
Institute of Architects

1993 National Honor Award
Morton International Building
American Institute of Architects

1993 Honor Award
Perry Community Education Village
Cleveland Chapter of the American
Institute of Architects

1993 Citation
Solon Middle School/Parkside
Elementary School
The American School and
University

1993 Interior Architecture Award
A.T. Kearney, Inc.
Chicago Chapter of the American
Institute of Architects

1993 Chicago Atheneum/IBD Award
A.T. Kearney, Inc.
Chicago Atheneum, "New Chicago
Interiors"

1993 Merit Award
Gwinnett Medical Center Women's
Pavilion
Georgia Chapter American Institute
of Architects

1992 Citation
Troy High School
The American School and
University

1992 Distinguished Building Award
Troy High School
Chicago Chapter of the American
Institute of Architects

1992 Honor Award
Solon Middle School/Parkside
Elementary School
Cleveland Chapter of the American
Institute of Architects

1992 Merit Award
Atlanta International School
American Institute of Architects,
South Atlantic Region

1991 Honor Award
Warsaw Community High School
Indiana Society of Architects

1991 Distinguished Building Award
Morton International Building
Chicago Chapter of the American
Institute of Architects

1991 Interior Architecture Award
Morton International Building
lobby
Chicago Chapter of the American
Institute of Architects

1991 Merit Award
Atlanta International School
Georgia Chapter, American
Institute of Architects

1990 National Honor Award
Capital High School, Santa Fe New
Mexico
American Institute of Architects

1990 Merit Award
Tarry Research and Education
Building, Northwestern University
The American School and
University

1990 Distinguished Building Award
Capital High School, Santa Fe New
Mexico
Chicago Chapter of the American
Institute of Architects

1990 Distinguished Building Award
Waste Management Environmental
Monitoring Laboratory
Chicago Chapter of the American
Institute of Architects

1990 Merit Award
Emory University Hospital Visitor
Reception Center
American Institute of Architects,
South Atlantic Region

1989 Distinguished Building Award
Orland Park Village Center
Chicago Chapter of the American
Institute of Architects

1989 National Honor Award
Desert View Elementary School
American Institute of Architects

1989 Honor Award
Emory University Hospital
Expansion and Renovation
Modern Healthcare

1989 Contract Design Award
Offices of Perkins & Will
Institute of Business Design/
Interior Design Magazine

1988 Honorable Mention
Desert View Elementary School
American Association of School
Administrators

1988 Honorable Mention
Capital High School,
Santa Fe New Mexico
American Association of School
Administrators

1988 Distinguished Building Award
Desert View Elementary School
Chicago Chapter of the American
Institute of Architects

1987 Citation
Warsaw High School
The American School and
University

1987 Certificate of Merit
Capital High School
Association of School Building
Officials

1986 Citation
Capital High School
The American School and
University

1985 Citation of Merit Award
Gwinnett Medical Center
Georgia Chapter of the American
Institute of Architects

1984 Architectural Design Award
Music Center, Pacific Lutheran
University
Progressive Architecture Awards
Program

1981 First Place
Al-Mustasiriyah Medical College and
Teaching Hospital Competition

**1978 Award of Merit for Unbuilt
Architecture**
Quarterback Tower
(Birmingham, Alabama)
Chicago Chapter of the American
Institute of Architects

Bibliography

"Morton International Building," *A+U*, April 1992, 118–26.

"Ingalls Memorial Hospital, Wyman-Gordon Pavillion," *A+U*, May 1984, 91–97.

"Recent High Rise Building in U.S.A.," *A+U*, October 1982, 101.

"Corporate Headquarters for Solor-Ray Systems Inc.," *A+U*, August 1982, 110–11.

Almada, Jeanette, "Westward Ho! Tower beyond expressway will serve as Greektown catalyst," *Chicago Tribune*, January 17, 1999, Section 16, 5.

A.I.A. Honor Awards, Perry Community Education Village, Perry, Ohio. *Architecture*, May 1996, 195.

"Lighting Controls," (Fallon McElligott) *Archi-Tech*, Fall 1998, 33.

Architectural Portfolio 1995. *American School & University Magazine*, November 1995, 50.

"AMA Tower, Manila, Philippines," *Architectural Record*, July 1996, PR2.

"The CORE Center, Chicago, Illinois," *Architectural Record*, July 1999.

"Sharon Hospital," *Architectural Record*, May 1997.

Linn, Charles. "Form Follows Flight," *Architectural Record*, June 1994, 114–27.

"New Architecture School Will Site at Campus Crossroad," *Architectural Record*, June 1993, 21.

"A Kit of Indigenous Design Parts," *Architectural Record*, December 1988, 101.

"Inventive Regionalism Sparks a Prototype for the Desert," *Architectural Record*, September 1988, 106–09.

"A Hybrid Hospital and Home." *Architectural Record*, June 1983, 98–101.

"Troy High School," *Architecture*, May 1994, 111.

"A Suburban High School Responds to Site Geometrics," *Architecture*, March 1994, 39.

"Morton International Building," *Architecture*, May 1993, 94.

"Waste Management Environmental Monitoring Laboratory," *Architecture*, July 1991, 85.

"Perry Community Education Village," *Architecture*, January 1991, 27.

"Byucksan Mixed-use Building," *Architecture + Interior Design*, (Korea) April 1993, 80–81.

"Architects Series No. 15: Ralph Johnson," *Architecture + Interior Design*, (Korea) June 1992, 141–63.

"Dongbu Central Research Institute," *Architecture + Interior Design*, (Korea) November 1991, 48–49.

"Architecture in the Public Realm," *Architecture Chicago Volume 13*, 1995, 15, 90–91, 112–13.

"Ralph Johnson 2 Chicago," *Architektura Bizens* (Warsaw) October, 1998, 16–19.

Armando, Diego. "El Legado de Dudok," *El Cronista Arquitectura & Diseno*, (Buenos Aires) May 1993, 1–2.8.

Arnaboldi, Mario. "A New Terminal in Chicago," *L'Arca*, April 1996, 74–79.

"*Plegeeinheiten in Krankenhausern*," *Baumeister*, February 1985, 60.

"*Die neuen Woldenkratzer in den U.S.A.*" *Baumeister*, February 1984, 55.

"123 North Wacker Drive, 100 North Riverside Plaza," *Bauwelt*, October 1989, 1930–35.

Bey, Lee. "Notebaert Nature Museum is a Harmonic Convergence," *Chicago Sun-Times*, October 24, 1999.

"Concentrated Care." *Building Design and Construction*, May 1999.

Bierman, Lindsay. "International Terminal at O'Hare International Airport," *Architecture*, August 1993, 46–47.

Boudaille, Georges. *Biennale de Paris section architecture 1982: La modernite ou l'esorit du temps*. Paris: Editions L'Equerre 1982, 201.

Branch, Mark Aldenand Cherly Kent. "Now Arriving," *Progressive Architecture*, June 1993, 88–89.

Broto, Carles. "Education and Culture," (Barcelona, Spain) *Links International*, 1997, 60–69.

"Sears Constructs a New Corporate Culture," *Building Operating Management*, 1994.

Bruegmann, Robert. "Local Asymmetrics," *Inland Architect*, March/April 1991, 43–49.

Bruegmann, Robert. "The Rationalist Tradition," *Inland Architect*, March/April 1991, 50–53.

Bruegmann, Robert. "Little Journeys to the Offices of Architects," *Inland Architect*, May/June 1983, 28.

Burgussoff, Nicolai. "All in One," *Architectural Record*, July 1995, 76–85.

Burkhardt, Francois Lieux. *De Travail*, Paris: Centre Georges Pompidou 1986, 22–23.

Busch, Jennifer. "Flying First," *Contract*, November 1995, 44–47.

Campbell, Jessica. "Temple Hoyne Buell Hall," *Ricker Notes*, School of Architecture, The University of Illinois, January 1996, 2-5.

Chek Lap Kok Airport *Gebaute Transparenz* (Germany), Ernst Wasmuth Verlag, 2000, 70–71.

The Chicago Architecture Annual, 1987. Chicago: Metropolitan Press Publications, 1987, 208–19.

The Chicago Architecture Annual, 1986. Chicago: Metropolitan Press Publications 1986, 214–19.

The Chicago Architecture Annual, 1985. Chicago: Metropolitan Press Publications 1985, 186–95.

"100 N. Riverside Plaza, Chicago, Illinois," *The Chicago Architectural Journal 8*, 1989, 186-87.

"A Civic Complex, Orland Park, Illinois," *The Chicago Architectural Journal 7*, 1988, 176–77.

"Office Building Hotel Complex, Chicago, Illinois," *The Chicago Architectural Journal 6*, 1987, 102–3.

The Chicago Architectural Journal 5, 1985, 150-51.

The Chicago Architectural Journal 4, 1984, 88.

The Chicago Architectural Journal 3, 1983, 60, 109.

"Brookville Hospital," *The Chicago Architectural Journal 2*, 1982, 90–91.

"The Chicago 100," *Chicago Tribune*, May 18, 1997.

"Attractive and Affordable Housing Keeps Students on Campus," *College Planning and Management*, May, 1998, 62.

Collyer, Stanley. "Ralph Johnson," *Competitions*, Winter 1995/96, 52–61.

Conroy, Connie. "The Next Generation: Workby Young Architects," *Inland Architect*, November/December 1985, 35.

"Bringing Space to Life–Ralph Johnson," *Contract Design*, May 1997, 140.

"Finally a Face," (Sharon Hospital) *Contract Design,* June 1996.

Cramer, Ned. "On the Boards: Project Portfolio, Perkins & Will," *Architecture*, February 1998, 46–47.

Dattner, Richard. *Civil Architecture–The New Public Infrastructure*, New York: McGraw-Hill 1995/96.

Deutsch, Randall, "The Prince of Thieves," *Focus Architecture Chicago*, October 1996, 17–18.

"Singapore American School, The Woodlands, Singapore 1993-1996" *Dialogue*, October 1997, 42–47.

Dibar, Carlos. "La Torre Morton de Chicago," *El Cronista Arquitectura & Diseno*, (Buenos Aires), December 1992, 1, 7, 8.

Dietsch, Deborah. "A Degree of Design Innovation on Campus," *Interiors*, December 1983, 32.

Dillon, David. "Contrasting Pair of El Paso Schools," *Architecture*, August 1988, 78–80.

Dixon, John Morris. "Confident Times Revisited," *Progressive Architecture*, July 1991, 94–99.

"Chicago: La griglia l'infinito." *Domus*, March 1982, 23.

Dorigati, Remo. "Temple Hoyne Buell Hall," *L'Arca*, May 1997, 34–41.

Dumaine, Brian. "Architects for the 1990s," *Fortune*, June 22, 1987, 159.

Dunlop, Beth. "North Fort Myers High School, North Fort Myers, Florida," *Architectural Record*, October 1997, 114–117.

"The 1987 Esquire Register," *Esquire*, December 1987, 106.

"Building for the Future," *Exchange Alumni Magazine, Duke, The Fuqua School of Business,* Fall 1998.

Fisher, Thomas. "The Place of Government," *Progressive Architecture*, October 1990, 65–77.

Fisher, Thomas. "Presenting Ideas," *Progressive Architecture*, August 1989, 78–81.

Fisher, Thomas. "Desert High," *Progressive Architecture*, August 1989, 78-81.

"Distinguished Building Award," *Focus*, October 1995, 8-9.

"Temple Hoyne Buell Hall," *Focus Architecture Chicago* September, 1998, 12.

Forth, Karl D. "Millwork: Team Concepts Boosts Productivity," (Martin/Williams), *FDM*, April 1999, 40-49.

Freeman, Alan. "A Tale of Four New Towers and What They Tell Us of Trends," *Architecture*, May 1988, 125-31.

Freiman, Ziva. "Neocon 92: Place for Homework," *Progressive Architecture*, August 1992, 14.

Gapp, Paul "A Brawny Chicagoan, Design of Morton International Building Accomplishes Daring Feats," *Chicago Tribune*, September 22, 1991, Section 6.20.

Gapp, Paul. "As Classy as 123, New Building Enhances Wacker-Franklin Strip," *Chicago Tribune*, February 15, 1987, Section 13.10.

Globota, Ante. *Chicago, 150 Years of Architecture, 1833-1983*, Paris: Paris Art Center 1983, 185-86, 231.236.

"International Terminal, O'Hare International Airport, Chicago," *Habbitat Ufficio*, April/May 1994, 44-53.

Hamilton, Joan et. al. "The New Workplace," (Fallon McElligott) *Business Week*, April 19, 1996, 107, 109,110.

"Center gets to the CORE of AIDS Issue," *Health Facilities Management*, August 1999.

"Modernism: Is It Still Alive?" *Inland Architect*, May/June 1984, 17.

"Worlds Fair Charrettes: A Look at Concepts for 1992," *Inland Architect*, March/April 1984, 46.

"Architecture and the Museum," *Inland Architect*, March/April 1983, 27.

"Pluralism's Poses," *Inland Architect*, July/August 1982, 38.

"Perkins & Will—Four Years After..." cover feature, *Interiors*, June 1993.

"Combining High Tech and De Still in a New Office Tower," *Interiors*, May 1988, 78.

Johnson, Ralph. "Universal, Yet Contextual," *Habbitat Ufficio*, April/May 1993, 2.

Johnson, Ralph. "Crow Island School." *Metropolitan Review*, November/December 1989, 48-49.

Johnson, Ralph. "Type, Program & Place: Four Projects," *University of Tennessee Journal of Architecture II*, 1989, 34-39.

Johnson, Ralph. "SolorRay Headquarters." *Threshold 1: The Journal of the Chicago School of Architecture*, The University of Illinois at Chicago 1982, 12-14.

"Proceedings from the Eighth Symposium on Healthcare Design, The Center for Health Design," *Journal of Healthcare Design, Volume VIII*, 1996.

Kamin, Blair. "Natural Beauty," *Chicago Tribune*, November 2, 1999.

Kamin, Blair, "Building Block," *Chicago Tribune*, Friday, February 20, 1998, Section 7, 3.

Kamin, Blair. "Structural Damage," *Chicago Tribune*, January 21, 1996, Section 7, 17.

Kamin, Blair. "Towering Success," *Chicago Tribune*, November 26, 1995, Section 7, 1, 16, 17.

Kamin, Blair. "Design," *Chicago Tribune*, October 7, 1995, Section 7.

Kamin, Blair. "Human Nature," *Chicago Tribune*, February 5, 1995.

Kamin, Blair. "O'Hare's New Face," *Chicago Tribune*, May 30, 1993, Section 13, 12-13.

Keegan, Edward. "Prairie Companion," *Architecture*, August 1996, 96-103.

Kent, Cheryl, "A Clinic That Cares," *Chicago Tribune*, December 1, 1998, Section 5, 5.

The Contemporary Architecture of the World, High Rise Building/Skyscraper. (Korea) Kunchuk-Doseo Publishing Co. 1997, 102-105.

"Near Chicago." (Motorola MIMS) *L'Arca* March 1999.

"*Academie du Musique,* Pacific Lutheran University," *L'architecture d'Aujourd'hui*, October 1983, XLII-XLIII.

"*Les nouveaus gratte-ciel Americains: la cinquieme generation,*" *L'Architecture d'Aujourd'hui*, April 1982, 75.

Litt, Steven. "Collegiate Modern," *Architecture*, November 1995, 100-105.

Madigan, M. J. "17th Annual Interiors Awards Competition Best Large Office," *Interiors Magazine,* January 1996, 48.

"International Terminal at O'Hare Airport," *Metropolitan Review,* May/June 1990, 66–73.

"Desert View Elementary School, Santa Fe High School, Perry Community Education Village," *Metropolitan Review,* September/October 1989, 90–99.

"123 Wacker Drive," *Metropolitan Review,* Summer 1988, 88–91.

Mullen, William. "New Day, Digs for Historic Museum," *Chicago Tribune,* April 21, 1997, Section 2, 3.

Nereim, Anders. "A Cathedral of Learning," *Architectural Record,* January 1991, 68–71.

Nelson, Susan. "Rising Stars," *Focus Architecture Chicago,* May 1997, 7.

Nesmith, Lynn. "Bioscience/Parks Hall Addition," *Architecture,* March 1993, 33.

Pastier, John. "Skyscraper Revolution and Evolution," *Design Quarterly 140,* 1988, 20–21.

Pearson, Cliff. "Urban Collage," *Architectural Record,* October 1993, 100–101.

Pearson, Cliff. *School Ways: The Planning and Design of America's Schools.* New York: McGraw Hill 1993, 84–86, 93–95, 122–25, 156, 179–81.

Pearson, Clifford. "Prairie Tech," *Architectural Record,* January 1991, 94–97.

Perry Community Education Village, Education & Culture, *Barcelona, Links International,* 1998, 60–69

Petersen, Laurie. "Site Seeing: A Grand Tour of Local Design Award Winners," *Focus Architecture Chicago,* November 1997, 13.

Phillips, Alan. "WMI Environmental Monitoring Laboratory," *The Best in Industrial Architecture,* New York: Watson-Guptill Publications 1990, 112–13.

"Making A Space for Architecture," *Progressive Architecture,* December 1995, 31.

"Office Building, Chicago, Illinois," *Progressive Architecture,* February 1985, 47.

"P/A Plans: Schools," *Progressive Architecture,* March 1993, 96–97, 101–2.

"Music Center Pacific Lutheran University," *Progressive Architecture: 31ˢᵗ Annual P/A Awards,* January 1984, 88–91.

"In Progress (100 Riverside, Orland Park)," *Progressive Architecture Record,* July 1988, 37, 41.

Ralph Johnson of Perkins & Will–Buildings & Projects. New York: Rizzoli, 1995.

Saliga, Pauline (ed.) *The Sky's the Limit: A Century of Chicago Skyscrapers.* New York: Rizzoli International Publications 1990, 270–71, 292.

"Architecture + Environment," *Sears Merchandise Group Headquarters,* June 1994.

Solomon, Richard Jay. "The Familiar Face of 123 North Wacker," *Inland Architect,* May/June 1988, 49-53.

"A.I.A. Firm of the Year '99 Perkins & Will" *Space* (Korea) January, 1999, 38–65.

Stucch, Silvano. "Riverside School in Sunland Park, New Mexico," *L'industria delle costruzioni,* 32–37.

Stein, Karen "School Spirit," *Architectural Record,* August 1993, 96–101.

581 Architects in The World. Tokyo: Toto Shuppan 1995, 362.

Tigerman, Stanley. *Chicago Architecture in the New Zeitgeist: In Search of Closure.* Lisbon: Fundacao Calouste Gulbenkian 1989, 106–7.

Turner, Nicola. "Ground Control," *World Architecture,* September 1999.

Twardy, Chuck. "Design Watch," *The Raleigh News & Observer,* December 7, 1996.

Twardy, Chuck. "The Urban Image," *The Raleigh Nes & Observer,* June 28, 1992.

"Research Triangle Park, NC," *Spectator Magazine,* June 4, 1992.

The Art of Architecture. University of Illinois at Urbana-Champaign, School of Architecture, 1995, 34–35.

"Egypt CIRD Nile Gateway Centre," *World Architecture,* June 1999.

Zukowsky, John. *Building for Air Travel.* Munich: Prestel Verlag 1996, 88, 92, 136, 187.

Zukowsky, John. *Chicago Architecture and Design, 1923–1993.* Munich: Prestel Verlag 1993, 348, 364, 418, 429.

Project Credits

SCHOOLS

Desert View Elementary School
Client: Gadsden Independent School District

Associate Architect: Mimbres, Inc.

Design Principal: Ralph E. Johnson

Project Architects: Kas Germanas, Sam Jamron

Project Manager: James Toya

Project Deisgner: John Arzarian, Jr.

Project Team: Elizabeth Fakatselis, Mark Romack, Jerry Johnson, Stuart Royalty, Pamela Kurz, Carolyn Smith

Troy High School
Client: Troy Public Schools

Design Principal: Ralph E. Johnson

Managing Principal: C. William Brubaker

Project Manager: James Toya

Project Deisgner: John Arzarian, Jr.

Project Team: Eric Spielman, Mike Hoffman, Geoffrey Brooksher, Elizabeth Fakatselis, Susan Emmons, Robin Randall, George Witaszek

Perry Community Education Village
Client: Perry Local School District

Associate Architect: Burgess & Niple, Ltd

Managing Principal: Ralph E. Johnson

Project Director: Raymond Bordwell

Project Manager: James Toya

Technical Coordinator: James Nowak, William Schmalz

Project Deisgners: August Battaglia, James Woods

Project Team: Eric Spielman, Mike Palmer, Jerry Johnson, Robin Randall, Robert Ruggles, Celeste Robbins, Carlos Parilla, Gregory Bennett, Randy Takahashi

North Fort Myers High School
Client: Lee County School Board

Associate Architect: Parker/Mudgett/Smith Architect, Inc.

Managing Principal: C. William Brubaker

Design Principal: Ralph E. Johnson

Project Manager: James Woods

Project Designer: Jerry Johnson

Project Team: Celeste Robbins, Steve Roberts, Thomas Vecchio

Illustrations: Brian Junge

Chelsea High School
Client: Chelsea School District

Associate Architect: Symmes Manni McKee Architects

Project Director: Edward Frenette

Managing Principal: C. William Brubaker

Design Principal: Ralph E. Johnson

Project Director: Ruth Gless

Project Architect: Michael Poynton

Project Programmer: Raymond Bordwell

Project Team: Steve Roberts, Wendy Gill, Michael Poynton, Tom Ahleman, Elias Vavaroutsos, Brian Junge

International School Beijing–Shunyi
Client: International School Beijing-Shunyi

Associate Architect: Beijing Institute of Architectural Design & Research

Principal in Charge: Ray Bordwell

Project Managers: Amy Yurko, Charles Alexander

Design Principal: Lisa Gould

Project Designer: Ron Vitale

Project Architect: David Cerruti, Peter Brown (Housing)
Project Team: John Gerney (Cadd Manager), Kevin Rice, Marina deConciliis, Benjamin Gilmartin, Mike Poynton, Peggy Hoffman (Interiors & FF&E), Stephen Sharlach (Signage) David Powell , Mark Bastian

International School of Manila
Client: International School of Manila

Associate Architect: J. T. Manosa & Associates

Design Principal: Ralph E. Johnson

Managing Principal: Raymond Bordwell

Senior Designer & Project Director: Amy Yurko

Project Architect: Mike Poynton

Project Team: Brian Meade, Nicola Casciato, Kimberly Brown, Tim Bicknell, Scott Kuehn, Brook Potter, Joe Pullara, Peggy Hoffmann

Illustrations: Nicola Casciato

Fearn Elementary School
Client: West Aurora School District

Principal in Charge: Gaylaird Christopher

Managing Principal: Steven Turckes

Design Director: John Dale

Project Director/Project Architect: Peter Brown

Project Team: Michael Palmer, Al Fitzpatrick, Peggy Hoffman, Anna Harvey, Kemba Mazloomian, George Beach, Ray Coleman, Binh Wong

Drawings: Tony Hensley, Sung Lee

Charter School
Client: Prologue

Design Principal: Ralph E. Johnson

Managing Principal: Steven Turckes

Project Architect: Peter Brown

Project Team: George Beach, Thomas Mozina, Todd Accardi

Illustrations: Gregory Geslicki

HIGHER EDUCATION

Temple Hoyne Buell Hall
Client: University of Illinois, Urbana–Champaign/ Capital Development Board

Design Principal: Ralph E. Johnson

Managing Principal: John Nunemaker

Project Manager: Scott Reed

Technical Coordinator: Robert Gross

Project Designer: Vojo Narancic

Project Team: Steve Turckes, Gary Jaeger, Dean Huspen, Thomas Vecchio

Monroe Community College
Client: Monroe Community College

Principal in Charge: Mark Chen

Project Manager: Ed Narbutas

Project Designer: Fred Alvarez

Project Architect: Ed Gulamarian

Project Team: Ron Vitale, Pat Daley, William van Horn

Emory University, North Decatur Building
Client: Emory University

Principal-in-Charge: Bill Viehman

Project Manager: Barbara Crum

Project Designer: James Smith

Emory University, Cox Hall

Client: Emory University

Principal-in-Charge: Henry Mann

Design Architect: Barbara Crum

Project Architect: Rebecca Higginbotham

Fuqua School of Business Student Center, Duke University

Client: Duke University

Principal in Charge: Philip A. Shive

Project Architect: James W. Merriman

Technical Architect: H. Michael Hill

Interior Designer: John R. Morris

Project Team: Richard S. Kazebee, James L. Kirby, John B. Boehms, G. Phillip Ingold

University of Miami School Of Communication

Client: University of Miami

Principal in Charge: Jose Gelabert-Navia

Project Designers: Jose Gelabert-Navia, Pat Bosch

Project Manager: Pat Bosch

Project team: Nora Hurtado, Rodrigo Carrion, Rodrigo Reyes, Alison Antrobus, Jack Superson, Miguel Fernandez

University of Chicago Graduate School of Business Competition

Client: University of Chicago

Design Principal: Ralph E. Johnson

Managing Principal: Joseph Chronister

Senior Designer: Thomas Mozina

Project Team: Khai Toh, Philip Hung, Cengiz Yetken, Gregory Geslicki

UCSD School of Medicine Neighborhood Planning Study

Client: University of California, San Diego

Project Architect/Director: John Dale

Principal/Contract Administrator: Michael Fejes

Project Planner: Mark Hartmann

Project Designer: Binh Wong

Miami Dade Community College, Aviation Training Center

Client: Miami Dade County Public Schools

Principal in Charge: Jose Gelabert-Navia

Project Designer: Pat Bosch

Project Manager: Carlos Chiu

Project Team: Luis Silva, Giselle Coujil, Miguel Quismondo, Giovanni Medina, Hector Solis

George Mason University

Client: George Mason University

Associate Architect: PageSutherlandPage

Principal Designer: Ralph E. Johnson

Project Director: Bridget Lesniak

Senior Designer: Gregory Geslicki

Project Team: Todd Snapp, Jeff Olson, Ken Soch

LABORATORIES

Tarry Research & Education Building, Northwestern University

Client: Northwestern University

Lab Planners: Earl Walls Associates

Design Principal: Ralph E. Johnson

Managing Principal: John E. Nunemaker

Interior Design Principal: Neil P. Frankel

Project Manager: James Tworek

Technical Coordinator: Robert Goldstead

Project Designer: Elizabeth Fakatselis

Project Team: Jerry Johnson, Pamela Kurz, Kevin O'Connor, George Witaszek, Falamak Norzed

Vernal G. Riffe, Jr. Building, Ohio State University

Client: The Ohio State University

Associate Architect: Burgess & Niple, Ltd.

Design Principal: Ralph E. Johnson

Managing Principal: Jeffrey Conroy

Project Manager: Chester Turner

Laboratory Planner: Jerry Clubb

Senior Technical Coordinator: Joseph Chronister

Senior Designer: Kurt Finfrock

Project Designer: Thomas Mozina

Project Team: Julie Evans, George Witaszek, Henry Lee

Dongbu Central Research Institute

Client: Dongbu Corporation

Design Principal: Ralph E. Johnson

Managing Principal: Donghoon Han

Project Designers: Cengis Yetkin, Aric Lasher

Project Team: Amy Yurko, Waleed Shalan, Wendy Gill, Tom Ahleman, Elias Vavaroustsos, Brian Jung

Biomedical Research Building II, University of Pennsylvania

Client: University of Pennsylvania

Associate Architect: Francis Cauffman, Foley Hoffman Architects, Ltd., Neil Hoffman, Executive V.P.

Lab Planners: GPR Planners Collaborative Inc.

Design Principal: Ralph E. Johnson

Managing Principal: John E. Nunemaker

Senior Designer: Jerry Johnson

Senior Technical Coordinator: Bill Schmalz

Project Team: Geoff Brooksher, Laurie Schwalb, Lawrence Dick, Elias Vavaroustsos, David Dunn, Bryan Schabel, Patrick McGuire, James Vira

McDonnell Pediatric Research Building, Washington University in St. Louis

Client: Washington University in St. Louis School of Medicine

Associate Architect: Mackey Michell Associates

Lab Planners: GPR Planners Collaborative Inc.

Design Principal: Ralph E. Johnson

Managing Principal: John E. Nunemaker

Project Manager: Paul Clinch

Project Designer: Jerry Johnson

Senior Project Architect: Bill Schmalz, Geoffrey Brooksher

Project Team: Elias Vavaroutsos, David Dunn, Thomas Czyzyk, James Vira, Scott Cyphers, Bryan Schabel

UCLA Neurosciences Institute

Client: University of California - Los Angeles

Lab Planners: GPR Planners Collaborative Inc.

Design Principal: Ralph E. Johnson

Senior Designer: Louis Raia

Project Manager: Paul Clinch

Project Architects: Thomas Braham, Fred Afshari

Project Team: Bryan Schabel, David Powell, Philip Hung, Nathalie Belanger, Jack Bransfield, Monica Oller, Raymond Coleman

Georgia Institute of Technology, Manufacturing Related Disciplines Complex Phase II
Client: Georgia Institute of Technology

Lab Planners: SST Planners

Principal-in-Charge: Bill Viehman

Design Principal: Manuel Cadrecha

Project Manager: Daniel Watch

Project Manager: Gary McNay

Project team: Kimberly Polkinhorn, Michael Reid , Karl Hirschmann

University of Southern California Neurogenetic Institute
Client: University of Southern California

Lab Planners: RFD Planners

Design Principal: Ralph Johnson

Managing Principal: Eric Aukee

Project Managers: Bridget Lesniak, Victor DeSantis

Senior Designer: Thomas Mozina

Project Team: Khai Toh, JC Sanchez, Jeff Olson, Michael Bowers, Ray Coleman

Thomas Jefferson University Cancer Center
Client: Thomas Jefferson University

Associate Architect: Francis Cauffman, Foley Hoffman Architects, Ltd.

Lab Planners: GPR Planners Collaborative Inc.

Design Principal: Ralph E. Johnson

Managing Principal: Terrence M. Owens

Principal Planner: Jocelyn Frederick

Senior Designer: Gregory Geslicki

Project Team: Rick Reindel

HEALTHCARE
Piedmont Hospital Rehabilitation and Fitness Center
Client: Piedmont Hospital

Principal in Charge: Lewis Nix

Project Designer: Barbara Crum

Hackensack Medical Center, Don Imus/ WFAN Pediatric Center for Tomorrow's Children
Client: Hackensack Medical Center

Managing Principal: Joseph Shein

Planning Principal: Donald Blair

Design Director: Audrey Matlock

Senior Designers: Tim Love, Lisa Gould
Project Manager: David Wilklow
Project Architects: Georgine Ilesco, David Whitaker
Project Team: Pat Daly, Mimi Garza, Jose Madrigal, James Huey, Richard Mariano, Joanne Violante, Lou Bauko, Bennett Reed, Raphael Neja, KK Tey

Sharon Hospital
Client: Sharon Hospital

Principal in Charge: Don Blair

Principal in Charge-Interiors: Neil Frankel

Project Designer: Lisa Gould

Project Manager: Thomas Lurcott

Project Architects: Carlo Panfilo, Polly Carpenter

Project Team: Tama Duffy, Richard Brennan, Barry Shapiro, Mimi Garza

South Georgia Medical Center, Pearlman Cancer Center
Client: South Georgia Medical Center

Principal in Charge: David Johnson

Project Manager: Jim Bynum

Design Architect: James Smith

Florida Hospital, Heartland Medical Center
Client: Florida Hospital

Principal in Charge: Lewis Nix

Project Manager: Phil Harrison

Design Architect: Manuel Cadrecha

Project Manager: Chris Tidwell

Project Planner: Leslie Saunders

MidState Medical Center
Client: MidState Medical Center
Partner in Charge: Don Blair

Partner in Charge - Interiors: Tama Duffy

Project Director: Dan Fenyn

Project Managers: Ed Narbutas, Charles Alexander

Design Principal: Lisa Gould

Project Designer: Ron Vitale
Project Architect: David Cerruti
Project Team: Carolyn BaRoss (Senior Interior Designer), Mark Leininger (Senior Planner), John Gerney (Cadd Manager), Judy Lee, Diane Fischer, Mason Wickham, Ana Stein (interiors), Edwin Zawadski, Leonard Composano, Juliet Alcancia

University of Illinois at Chicago Ambulatory Care Facility
Client: University of Illinois at Chicago

Design Principal: Ralph E. Johnson

Managing Principal: Jocelyn Frederick

Project Manager: Larry Kettleson

Project Architect: Milan Miladinovich

Interior Designer: Charles Sheppard

Project Team: Jerry Quebe, Rick Reindel, Ben Kogan, Holly Roeske, Rachael Smith, Greg Brewer, Vojo Naranic, Mukhtar Khalil, John Hopkins, Diane Love, Pam Crowell, Todd Baisch, Linda Noggle, Geoffrey Brooksher, Lou Raia

UCLA, Health Sciences Campus 120-day Master Plan Study
Client: University of California Los Angeles

Associate Architects: Kohn Pederson Fox; Lee Burkhart Liu

Design Principal: Ralph Johnson

Managing Principal: Jean Mah

Project Designer: Tannys Langdon

Project Team: Bryan Schabel

The CORE Center AIDS/HIV Clinic
Client: Cook County Bureau of Health Services & Rush-Presbyterian- St. Luke's Medical Center

Associate Architect: Campbell, Tiu, Campbell

Design Principal: Ralph E. Johnson

Managing Principal: Jocelyn Frederick

Senior Designer: Jerry Johnson

Project Architect: Kurt Smith

Interior Designers: Allison Wojcik, Dennis St. John

Project Team: Jerry Quebe, Amy Yurko, Clark Fell, Brad Winklejohn, Charles Sheppard, Carolyn Schachtner, Angeline Karibian

CORPORATE OFFICE

Morton International Building
Client: Orix Real Estate Equities

Design Principal: Ralph E. Johnson

Managing Principal: James C. Allen

Project Manager: Charles Anderson

Senior Designer: August Battaglia

Project Designer: Mark Romack

Technical Coordinator: Joseph Pullara

Project Team: Jerry Johnson, John Karabatsos, Stuart Royalty, Steven Ward, Laura Alberga, Paul Hagle, Carlos Parilla, Mike Hoffman, Phil Zinny, Eric Spielman

Sears Integrated Business Headquarters and Expansion
Client: Sears Integrated Business

Design Principal: David Hansen

Managing Principal: John Nunemaker

Project Manager: James Lubawy

Senior Designer: Mike Henthorn

Senior Technical Coordinator: Bill Schmalz

Project Team: Geoff Brooksher, Peggy Hoffmann, David Brubaker, Philip Zini,

Keith Kreink, Maria Lewin, Michael Petty

Phase II Addition:

Design Principal: David Hansen

Managing Principal: James Lubawy

Project Manager: James Lubawy

Senior Designer: Randy Guillot

Senior Technical Coordinator(Design): Michael McGeady

Senior Technical Coordinator(Construction): Alex Wray

Project Team: Charles Killibrew, Tyler Shryer, Tim Bicknell

Site Supervision: John Jackowski

AMA Tower
Client: AMA Land—Daewoo Corporation, Engineering & Construction

Associate Architects: Luis & Associates

Design Principal: Ralph E. Johnson

Managing Principal: G. William Doerge

Project Manager: G. William Doerge

Project Architects: Thomas Demetrion, Thomas Mozina

Project Team: Brian Junge, David Poorman, Nicola Casciato

Grainger, Inc. Headquarters
Client: Grainger, Inc.

Interior Architect: The Environments Group

Design Principal: David Hansen

Managing Principal: Terrence M. Owens

Senior Designers: Michael Henthorn, Randy Guillot

Senior Technical Assistant: Jim Novak

Project Architects: John Bowers, Hans Thummel, Marty Jurasek

Project Team: David Powell, Michelle Fisher, Peggy Hoffmann, Todd Baisch

Burroughs Wellcome Fund
Client: Burroughs Wellcome Fund

Design Principal: Philip A. Shive

Project Manager: James W. Merriman

Interior Designer: John R. Morris

Technical Architect: H. Michael Hill

Project Team: John B. Boehms

North Carolina Biotechnology Center
Client: North Carolina Biotechnology Center

Principal in Charge: Philip A. Shive

Technical Architect: H. Michael Hilll

Interior Designer: John R. Morris

Motorola Office and Manufacturing Building
Client: Motorola

Design Principal: David Hansen

Principal in Charge: John Nunemaker

Senior Designer: Randy Guillot

Project Architect: Michael McGeady

Project Team: Larry Kettelson, Jeffrey Olson, Dianne Zabich, David Dunn

MetroBank Headquarters
Client: Metropolitan Bank

Design Principal: Ralph E. Johnson

Principal in Charge: G. William Doerge

Senior Designer: Nicola Casciato

Espirito Santo Bank Competition
Client: Espirito Santo Bank

Design Principal: Ralph E. Johnson

Managing Principal: G. William Doerge

Project Team: Nicola Casciato, Nathalie Belanger

LG Bundang Research and Development Complex
Client: LG Group

Associate Architect: Chang-Jo Architects

Principal in Charge: G. William Doerge

Design Principal: Ralph E. Johnson

Project Manager: Walter Heffernan

Project Designer: Cengiz Yetken

Project Team: Nicola Casciato, Thomas Mozina, David Powell, Charles Killebrew, George Beach, Nathalie Belanger, Monica Oller, Eric Spielman, David Poorman, Curt Behnke, James Prendergast, June Oh, Kathy Orser-Wendt, Jin Huh, Charles Sheppard

CIRD Headquarters
Client: CIRD

Associate Architect: Dar Al-Handasah (Shair and Partners)

Design Principal: David Hansen

Managing Principal: G. William Doerge

Senior Designer: Randy Guillot

Project Architect: Nathalie Belanger

Crate & Barrel Corporate Headquarters

Client: Crate & Barrel

Design Principal: Ralph E. Johnson

Managing Principals: G. William Doerge and Terrence M. Owens

Senior Designer: Hans Thummel

Project Team: Alex Wray, Terri Johnson, Bryan Schabel

Illustrations: Gregory Geslicki

CIVIC

Orland Park Village Center

Client: Village of Orland Park, Illinois

Design Principal: Ralph E. Johnson

Managing Principal: Terrence M. Owens

Project Manager: Charles Anderson

Project Designer: August Battaglia

Project Team: Carlos Parilla, Carolyn Smith, George Witaszek, Pamela Kurz, Robin Randall, Steven Ward

Field Team: Thomas Kamis, Ken Kloss

International Terminal, O'Hare International Airport

Client: City of Chicago, Department of Aviation & Department of Public Works

Associate Architects: Heard & Associates, Ltd./ Consoer Townsend & Associates

Design Principal: Ralph E. Johnson

Managing Principal: James M. Stevenson

Project Manager: James A. Economos

Senior Designer: August Battaglia

Project Planner: Mark Romack

Project Designer: Elizabeth Fakatselis

Project Team: Joseph Pullara, Jon Pohl, Mike Gillaspie, Mark Jolicoeur, Doug Grimm, Steve Bogay, Robert Ruggles, Dina Griffin, Paul Pettigrew, Thomas Kamis, Billy Tindel, Larry Robertson, Paul Hagle, Susan Barnes, Fred Afshari, Michael Poynton, Henry Lee, Bernie Woytek, Davor Engle, Phil Zinny

Chek Lap Kok Airport Competition

Client: Hong Kong Provisional Airport Authority

Managing Principal: James M. Stevenson

Design Principal: Ralph E. Johnson

Project Manager: Wally Bissonnette

Project Designer: August Battaglia

Project Planner: Mark Romack, Mark Jolicoeur

Project Team: Cengiz Yetken, Thomas Mozina, Aric Lasher

Peggy Notebaert Nature Center

Client: Chicago Academy of Sciences

Exhibit Design: Lee H. Skolnick Architecture + Design Partnership

Design Principal: Ralph E. Johnson

Project Director: Terrence M. Owens

Project Architect: Michael Poynton

Senior Designer: Thomas Mozina

Project Team: Nicola Casciato, Elias Vavaroutsos, Jeff Olson, Michael Bowers, Geoffrey Brooksher, David Poorman, Tyler Shyrer, Jerry Johnson, David Dunn

YMCA – Centennial Place

Client: YMCA

Principal in Charge: Bill Viehman

Project Designer: James Smith

Project Architect: Suzanne Blam

St. Mark's Catholic Church Competition

Client: Archdiocese of Miami

Principal in Charge: Jose Gelabert-Navia

Project Designer: Giselle Coujil

Project Team: Carlos Ramirez, Werner Gilles, Pat Bosch

Miami Beach Regional Library Competition

Client: City of Miami Beach

Principal in Charge: Jose Gelabert-Navia

Project team: Manuel Cadrecha, Amy Landesberg, Pat Bosch, Jose Bofill, Rodrigo Carrion, Rodrigo Reyes

John G. Shedd Aquarium

Client: John G. Shedd Aquarium

Exhibit Design: Shedd in-house exhibit team- Paul Bluestone, Brian Cavanaugh, Bryan Schuetze; & Lyons/Zaremba Inc.

Associate Architect: Perkins & Will - design consultant in association with Esherick, Homsey, Dodge and Davis

Design Principal: Ralph E. Johnson

Senior Designers: Curt Behnke, Cengiz Yetken

Project Team: Nicola Casciato, Khai Toh, Monica Oller, Philip Hung

HOUSING

Katherine and William Mayer Residences, Tulane University

Client: Tulane University

Associate Architect: Lyons & Hudson Architects

Design Principal: Ralph E. Johnson

Project Manager: Joseph Chronister

Project Designer: Nicola Casciato

Project Team: Keith Kreinik, Kimberly Brown, John O'Neil

NARA Towers & Marina

Client: Hardco

Associate Architect: Dar Al-Handasah (Shair & Partners)

Design Principal: Ralph E. Johnson

Project Manager: Walt Heffernan

Senior Designer: Vojo Narancic

Project Architect: Hans Thummel

Project Team: Randy Guillot, Charles Killebrew, George Beach, Mark Bastien, Curt Behnke, John Andrea

Ain El-Mreisseh Hotel and Marina

Client: Confidential

Associate Architect: Dar Al-Handasah (Shair & Partners)

Design Principal: Ralph E. Johnson

Managing Principal: G. William Doerge

Senior Designer: Thomas Mozina

Project Team: Philip Hung, Bryan Schabel, Nathalie Belanger

Skybridge at One North Halsted

Client: Dearborn Development

Design Principal: Ralph E. Johnson

Managing Principal: G. William Doerge

Project Manager: Terrence M. Owens

Senior Designer: Curt Behnke

Project team: Brian Junge, Ken Soch, Charles Killebrew, Monica Oller, Jack Bransfield, Aimee Mosesson

INTERIORS

A. T. Kearney

Client: A.T. Kearney

Managing Principal: Neil Frankel

Project Director: Barbara Falconer

Senior Designer: James Prendergast

Senior Technical Coordinator: Carol Simpson

Project Team: Erin Langland, Ray Viquez, Julie Carpenter

Martin/Williams Advertising and FAME

Client: **Martin /Williams, Inc**

Project Designer/Project Manager: Jim Young

Interior Designer: Beth Goeff

CADD Technician: Greg Fait

Fallon McElligott 29th Floor Office Expansion

Client: Fallon McElligott

Project Manager: Jim Young

Interior Designers: Amy Young, Heather Sheehan

Towers Perrin, Stamford

Client: Towers Perrin

Partner in Charge: John Lijewski (All Floors)

Senior Designer/Project Manager: William DeRidder (7th Floor)

Project Architect: Heriberto Camacho (7th Floor, PM/PA for floors 4–6)

Project Team (7th floor): Connie Pelina, Avery Handy, Jennifer Sowman

Project Team (floors 4-6): Jennifer Sowman, Carolyn BaRoss

Northwestern Medical Faculty Foundation

Client: Northwestern Medical Faculty Foundation

Managing Principal: Jocelyn Frederick

Project Manager: Bill Berger

Senior Designer: Art Krohnert

Project Team: Greg Brewer, Karin Deam, Carol Simpson, Todd Dundon, Allison Wojcek, Irris Ball, Jennifer McCoulouch, Scott Struik, Robert Cohoon

American Hospital Association

Client: American Hospital Association

Managing Principal: James Prendergast

Project Director: Tom Ruscetti

Project Team: Cynthia DeGrace, June Oh, Bill Berger, Jason Rosenblatt

Tribune Interactive

Client: Chicago Tribune

Design Principal: Ralph E. Johnson

Managing Principal: James Prendergast

Project Manager: Frank Pettinati

Project Team: Jason Rosenblatt, Nathalie Belanger, Lindsay Steinacher

Acknowledgments

Perkins & Will would like to express our appreciation to all our staff, both past and present, for their continued dedication to the pursuit of excellence in architecture. And, perhaps most importantly, we thank our clients for their on-going support and collaboration through the design process; together we have been able to translate architectural visions into reality.

Index

Bold page numbers indicate projects
included in Selected Works